Meant To Be

Marybeth Gills

Copyright © 2023 by Marybeth Gills

All rights reserved.

No portion of this book may be reproduced in any form without written permission from the publisher or author, except as permitted by U.S. copyright law.

contents

PROLOGUE: THE WEDDING	1
CHAPTER ONE: THE LOST BRIDE	6
CHAPTER TWO: THE RUNAWAY BRIDE	21
CHAPTER THREE: THE PLOT THICKENS	36
CHAPTER FOUR: STAYING ALIVE	51
CHAPTER FIVE: SILVER LININGS	66
CHAPTER SIX: JUST MISSED YOU	81
CHAPTER SEVEN: DOWN MEMORY LANE	96
CHAPTER EIGHT: LOVE WITHOUT MEMORY	111
CHAPTER NINE: TABLES ARE TURNED	126
CHAPTER TEN: WHAT THE HELL?	141
CHAPTER ELEVEN: KEEP ME SAFE	156
CHAPTER TWELVE: TO LOVE AGAIN	171

CHAPTER THIRTEEN: GOT YOU BACK	186
CHAPTER FOURTEEN: MOOT POINT	201
CHAPTER FIFTEEN: HIS PAST MISTAKE	215
CHAPTER SIXTEEN: INNOCENT UNTIL PROVEN GUILTY	230
CHAPTER SEVENTEEN: THE SURPRISE VISIT	245
CHAPTER EIGHTEEN: DANGER AHEAD	260
CHAPTER NINETEEN: DEAD OR ALIVE?	275
EPILOGUE: FINALLY YOURS...	290

PROLOGUE: THE WEDDING

Aidan stood looking in the mirror feeling his heart pound in his chest. One year ago, if somebody would have told him he would have ended up in marriage, he would have probably strangled that person. But now as he stood in his tuxedo, he felt none of the nervousness he should be feeling when he was going to face his worst fear. His commitment phobia.

Trying to stifle his impatience, he checked his reflection one last time and looked up at his best man for support.

"Ryce? Is she ready yet?" he asked for the tenth time. He was supposed to already waiting for her in the church but was being delayed because the bride was not ready yet.

"No, Jennifer just texted me. Kate is not ready yet," Ryce repeated and Aidan felt he was trying his patience.

But he could not help it. He was impatient to go to the church and make her his wife and she was not ready yet. Hell, why was she taking so much time to get ready. The Kate he knew would have been more eager than him and pressing him. He frowned. Was there something wrong?

"Put me through with Jennifer please," he said roughly feeling nervous now that something might not be happening like planned.

"Aidan! Relax. You wait here. I'm going to see what is wrong," Ryce almost ordered him but he was not fooling Aidan. He could pick up the worry in his best friend's tone even as he was trying not to show any of it. Damn!

Silently, he watched Ryce fled from the room to head in the direction of the north wing where Kate was getting ready. They had decided to get married in Manhattan itself where the castle was being used for their reception after the wedding ceremony. They were supposed to head for the nearby church where the minister must already be waiting for the groom.

But Jennifer had called asking Ryce to wait before they went to the church as Kate was not ready yet. And it was already one hour since her first call and in spite of all his phobia gone, Aidan could not help feeling a bit apprehensive. What the hell was going on?

Sighing, he sat on the nearby sofa. He had waited six months to be re-united with the love of his life so he could make it for another few minutes. Trying to keep busy, he got lost in a business magazine reading the latest stock figures which would help him later.

Ten minutes later, he flipped the magazine shut as he could hardly concentrate checking his watch for the hundredth time. There was still no news of Ryce now and he was starting to get worried. What the hell was going on? He knew he should go and find out but his mother must be guarding the door like a watchdog since he was not supposed to see his bride yet.

Another ten minutes later, he marched out of the door and headed to the north determinedly. As soon as he caught sight of his mother, the latter signaled him.

"Aidan? What are you doing here?" she whispered in a horrified tone pulling him towards the end of a corridor. "You are supposed to wait until we ask you to go to the church."

"I know but it's been more than one hour. I think the guests are waiting and I should go but my best man has disappeared and my bride is not ready yet," he said frowning at his mother when she blocked his way towards the door where Kate was getting ready.

"You can't go in there!" she cried outrageously. "You must not see the bride before the ceremony. It's bad omen."

"Mom, I have to see her. I'm sure there's something wrong!" he said setting his mother aside gently before barging into the room without giving his mother time to react this time.

As soon as he opened the door, everybody froze and he searched desperately for his bride in the room. Kate was nowhere to be seen and he felt panic starting to grab hold of his body.

"Aidan! What are you doing here?" asked Jennifer with Ryce right behind him.

"Where's Kate?" he rasped impatiently. "I need to see her now!" he said trying hard not to give in to the feeling of dread which was threatening to swallow him.

"She's in the washroom. She'll be here soon enough. Ryce, why don't you take Aidan to the church for the time being?" Jennifer addressed her husband but Aidan caught the look of alarm on his best friend's face and confirmed that something terribly wrong was happening.

Without waiting for anyone another attempt of convincing him otherwise, he dashed to the washroom and found the room empty as he had suspected. Kate was nowhere to be found.

"Where is she?" he barked furious that they were lying to him.

"Aidan, son. Please try to keep your calm." Alex got closer to him and placed his hand on his shoulder as guise of support. But he was beyond comforting at this stage.

"Just tell me where she is damn it!"

"We don't know. We have searched for her everywhere in the house but she cannot be found. She's gone," Alex announced in a dull voice.

"Gone?" he repeated like a parrot. "Gone?" he tried again but nothing came out except for the very same word.

"Aidan!" somebody cried in the background but he could no longer focus as his limp body fell down on the floor in shock. Kate was gone. And for the first time in his life, he felt his heart break into millions of pieces. There were so many questions in his mind right now that he thought he would just go crazy.

When was she gone? Where was she gone? Why was she gone? Hell!

CHAPTER ONE: THE LOST BRIDE

Still in deep shock, Aidan Waldorf could still not focus what was happening in reality. It was as if he had zapped out to another universe where his mind was bombarded with questions one after the other. Why was Kate no longer here? Where was she? Had she freaked out at the last minute and decided to skip the wedding? Or has something happened to her?

The only thing which kept him sane was the fact that Kate might be in some kind of danger and all he knew was that he had to find her. It was what his instincts were telling him and for the first time of his life, his heart was in synch with his mind. But it didn't make him feel better.

Standing up still in a daze, he ignored the noises around him and ran towards the door focusing only on what he was supposed to do. Only to be stopped by a pair of hands and he whirled round to see it was Ryce Vin Connor. His best friend. His brother.

But he was in no mood for the comfort Ryce as offering. It would serve no purpose until he had Kate with him. Nothing was making sense as he was having the constant zing in his head. Without saying a word, he shrugged off his hold and made for the door again. Only to be stopped by his mother who stood between the door and himself blocking his exit.

"Aidan, where are you going?" Meredith Waldorf shouted and he could only look back with unfocused eyes.

Suddenly, he felt his body shake and his teeth rattle. Snapping out of his daze, he saw that his mother had been shaking him and had repeated the question. Hell, where was he going? His ears were ringing and he could feel himself sway before slumping down on something he could hardly register.

"Find Kate," he mumbled his jaws feeling like lead. The initial shock had subsided and he no longer felt numb. But his initial instincts were still kicking in; Kate was in danger. He could feel it. Kate would never leave him like that without any plausible reason.

"Where??" Ryce growled and he looked up in the pair of grey eyes in front of him.

Where? Where what? Then he registered that Ryce had asked him where he was going. And he did not know where to go because he did not know where Kate was. The gravity of the situation finally dawned on him as he sat defeated on the sofa staring into space.

"We must inform the police," he finally heard the anxious tone of Alex Thornton his future father-in-law and he still looked up with a dazed expression. His mind was still lingering in the fact that Kate was no longer around. How would he be able to bear that?

What would he do without her? He had already kicked her out of his life before having taken her for granted and now that he knew how much she counted for him, she was gone. Life was so unfair sometimes.

"Are you alright?" his mother asked him and he nodded absent-mindedly. He was obviously not alright. But he could not let his misery apparent to anyone else; they were already as flustered as he was by the sudden disappearance of his bride.

"Aidan, love. I'm so sorry," Mrs. Judith Thornton was saying her eyes filled with tears. His mother in law was a nice person even if she got on his nerves sometimes but since she was close to her daughter, Aidan could never show her any disrespect. What he couldn't understand was why she was apologizing; she had nothing to do with the disappearance of her daughter, had she?

Suddenly as the idea bloomed in his mind, it stuck and wouldn't go away. Judith Thornton had never approved of their relationship. Not when she had wanted Kate to marry Edward Bigfoot. The son of her closest friend.

But Kate had never loved anyone else apart from him. Even since the university days and had agreed to marry Edward only to please her parents. Something which he could not resent since it had brought them together.

Frowning, he looked at her mother-in-law closely trying to decipher something in her expression. What if she had been the one who had asked Kate not to marry him? But why would her mother talk to her out of the marriage on his damned wedding day? Heaven knew how difficult it had been for them to finally be together.

It had been only after six months that they had become official with their relationship. Alex had asked him to wait for some time after the previous wedding had been cancelled. And Aidan had given his father-n-law his word that he would not see Kate for the coming seven months and he had kept his word. But Kate had not agreed with the deal.

Reluctant at first not to see for such a long time, she had finally acquiesced because she too had been worried what the world would think of her. Not that Aidan had given a damn.

But it had mattered to her and her family. And he had needed to prove how much she counted for him too and he had not wanted her reputation to be compromised at any cost. So no matter how hard it had been, he had left her and moved back to New York.

And had counted the days when he could finally meet his love. But after six months, every gossip about the cancelled wedding had died and he had felt it right to meet her again. He had been the only one who knew how difficult it had been to finally see her after such a long time. It had been a hell of a reunion and he had never had such an emotional high in his life.

Just when he had thought that he was going to get his forever and ever kind of ending, he had been left stranded on his wedding day. He didn't give a damn about the gossips or bad mouthed people who was sure to speculate on the lost bride.

No, he had seen worst in his life; he had grown up without a father and was made of tougher stuff than that. What mattered to him was Kate. What could break his heart was that if something major had happened to Kate. And he had a premonition that something like that was going to fall on him soon.

"Do you know anything?" he asked in a cold voice which made Judith freeze. "Anything at all?" he emphasized unaware that he was holding his breath and that his green eyes were as cold as ice as he stared in the woman's eyes.

"No, of course not! The last time I talked to her, she was smiling like never before. It was as if she was mad with happiness."

Her words made him release his breath. So he was not the only one who had noticed how happy Kate had been. Especially during the past two days. And that was why it was hard for him to believe that Kate had ran from him. She had loved him even when they had been best friends; even when he had been too dimwit to realize the true emotions he had for her.

Such kind of love could never be faked and he was damned sure that Kate must have left for a very specific reason. Unless she had been a really good actress. Which Aidan doubted. He had known her since she had been nineteen and there was no one so honest as her in the contemporary world. It was what had attracted him to her so damn much; her innocence and perseverance in life.

As he stared into the woman in front of him, he saw that Judith had no guilt written on her face and he cast the silly thought aside. How could a mother stop her own daughter's wedding especially since she had been saying that her daughter had looked happy?

"I'm sorry. I think I'm getting paranoid," he finally said and thankfully Judith dropped the matter refraining from any further comments.

Out of the corner of his eyes, he saw Ryce picked up his iPhone which had been ringing.

"Yes?" he barked right into the device as if it was the one responsible for the whole thing. "Okay, we're coming right away," he continued in the same brusque tone and disconnected the phone immediately.

"The police is here," he stated blandly to no one in particular.

There was a hush as everybody walked out of the room hurriedly but Aidan leant back with his eyes closed. He needed a few moments alone before getting back his strength. Hell, he felt like someone had cut off his right arm right now.

Where could she have gone? Had something happened to her? His headache was back with a vengeance and suddenly a thought occurred to him. What if she had never left on her own will? What if someone had broken into the house for some robbery and had seen her getting ready with expensive jewels? There was a wedding in the house and the security guards must have been careless.

Or worse? What if she had been kidnapped? Of course! There were several exits from the castle and not every one of them was guarded. That was a more plausible explanation to him and the more he thought about it, the more he was sure of his hunch.

But it was futile mopping around what had happened; if he wanted his Kate back, he had to get up like a man and find her. He had to be strong enough to survive this and be there for her when she would need him the most. If he found her. When he found her, he corrected himself with a new determination.

Feeling that he had to do something, he stood up and as he joined the others downstairs. As he reached the main lounge, he could hear Alex relating to the officers the headlines of the story. Headline being: the bride could not be found only one hour before the wedding ceremony. Which sounded lame even to himself.

The two burly police officers looked skeptical and wanted to know who was the last person who had talked to Kate before she was missing. After some questions, they discovered that it was her sister Caitlin who had been helping her fix her dress two hours before the ceremony.

"I was fixing her dress when I went to the attic room to fetch another set of pins. And you know how far the east wing is," she said as if talking to herself. Everybody nodded focusing on every detail. They were all in the same situation. Almost going crazy with worry.

Aidan knew that out of her three sisters, Kate was closest to Caitlin since the latter was only three or four years younger. The other two sisters were twins; Jade and June and were still in their early twenties still studying at university.

It was clear to him that Kate would never run from anyone in her family. She loved them too much for that.

"When I came back, she was not in the fitting room, I looked for her in the washroom but she was still nowhere to be found. And so I waited for her. Sure that she would come back because she had been wearing her wedding dress for Christ's sake. Where the hell would she go with that uncomfortable white dress?" Caitlin explained to the officer unable to stop the tears streaming down her face.

And Caitlin was right. If Kate had fled in her wedding dress, it would have seemed pretty weird. So, upon listening to everyone's story, he felt almost sure that she had been kidnapped. What other explanation could there be? Already feeling worry surge in his heart, he started to concentrate on who could the kidnapper be. Maybe Alex had an enemy who had abducted her daughter for some personal reasons? And he decided to share that piece of information with the cops.

"Exactly!" he said. "Somebody would have seen her running in a wedding dress. I think she has been kidnapped," he stated and there was a general audible gasp in the audience at his bold sentence.

"Are you sure?" asked Jade speaking for the first time since the ordeal.

"What other explanations could there be? She had left with only her wedding dress. With no money, no bag. Judith had checked her belongings. Everything was intact; even her honeymoon suitcase. It is clear that she had not planned this escapade," he stated firmly and everyone nodded.

"Now! Now! Let's not speculate about what happened for the time being," scolded the police officer whose name was Ryan Bridge. "So for how many hours did you wait?" he asked Caitlin turning back to her.

"I don't know. I waited for approximately thirty minutes when mom and the other girls joined me in the fitting room ready to help me with the bride," she stated and the focus shifted on the other three women.

"And ma'am what had you been doing in the meantime?" asked the other police officer whose tag name wrote Liam Curtin. Aidan could hardly suppress his rage; why were the officers wasting time asking stupid question when all they had to do was find Kate?

Ready to blast, he opened his mouth but promptly closed it when he felt a hand on his shoulder. It was Ryce again who stopped him by shaking his head in his direction having clearly read what was in his mind. Hell, what a bunch of losers!

The officers bombarded them with futile question wasting their time. How did the bride behave before the wedding? Has anybody detect anything at all in her usual behavior? What time was the ceremony scheduled for? What time was she supposed to get to church?

As predicted, everybody gave the same answers which left them with no trail and they asked one final question. Where were you when between noon and one? And each family member had an alibi. Since it was the wedding of such a close person, everybody had been getting ready for the wedding. When the police officers had finished talking to everyone, they saluted saying that they will keep in touch and Aidan ran after them.

"So, what are your plans to find Kate?" he asked being closely followed by Ryce.

"We're sorry. We cannot do anything for the time being."

"Huh? Excuse me?" Ryce asked snatching the words from his mouth before he had time to voice them out. What the hell did he mean that he could do nothing for the time being. What were they supposed to do?

"We have to follow the rules. A missing person can only be searched if he or she have been missing for twenny four hours," the officer Ryan drawled in a slurry voice which made Aidan want to punch his sorry face down.

"So, you're telling me that we have to wait for another day for you to start looking up for Kate?" he shouted. "But she had not taken anything with her. She must not be far away," he ranted his desperation clear now.

"Exactly. And we're pretty sure that it's no big deal. She must have run from the marriage and will be back before dawn."

That was it! How dared that sorry excuse of a man insult his relationship between him and Kate? Hell, he had no idea what they meant to each other. Aidan lifted his clenched fist ready to re-atomize his face when Ryce stopped him from behind once again.

"Aidan, stop! You don't want to end up in jail while Kate is missing, do you?" he hissed with fury and Aidan dropped his hand immediately. Ryce was right. It would serve no purpose if he landed up in jail while Kate was still in danger.

Gritting his teeth, he swallowed any insult which was threatening to come out before asking. "What about the possibility that she might have been kidnapped? Isn't that something you can explore for the time being?"

"No," replied Bridge. "If she has been kidnapped, there will be a demand for ransom and we have to wait for that before taking any initiative. We are at a moot point and can do nothing more, sir," he was informed and he stood still as he watched the two officers drive away.

How the hell was he supposed to sit back and wait for Kate when she could be in some serious and dangerous situation? Wasn't there a protocol for such type of situations? How could the cops be so.. so careless? As he stared at the retreating vehicle, he felt rage consume him and he wanted to throw something at the rear window.

"Come on!" Ryce called to him running to the Alex's truck. "Let's go and see if we can find her around. Like you said, she had nothing with her. No money. No car. And no luggage. She mustn't have gone too far."

Filled with hope, he hopped in the vehicle and they drove five times to in the nearby streets asking anybody if they had seen someone running in her wedding dress. Surprisingly, nobody had seen her and it was still broad daylight.

Maybe they had taken the wrong direction. They did the same for the other three directions but to no avail. It would have been too easy, thought Aidan derisively as he went back to the house looking and feeling defeated.

"Son, what happened?" asked Alex as he reached the doorstep. "Have you been able to find something? Anything?" and Aidan shook his head.

"No, we have driven till Central Park but nobody had seen her anywhere. It's as if she had disappeared into thin air. Which leads to only one explanation. She has been kidnapped," he said with conviction.

Alex nodded. "You're right. I have also been racking my brain for the past few hours and this seems to be the only explanation. What has the police said?"

"Nothing," Ryce intervened. "They can do nothing for the time being. Even if she has been kidnapped, they have to wait for the demand for ransom call before taking any actions. The police is convinced that Kate has ran because of the wedding," Ryce explained.

Alex frowned. "Because of the wedding?" he repeated uncomprehendingly. "What the hell is that supposed to mean?"

"They're saying that it's nothing serious. That she will be back before dawn as she has been having second thoughts about the wedding."

"How dare they talk like that about my daughter?" Alex fumed. "I've never heard of such absurdities. Don't worry boys. Let me call the superintendent Gregory Kyle. He's my friend and he might be in a better position to help us out."

It was a silver lining among the suddenly grey clouds and he was ready to grasp straws if it meant that he would find something about Kate.

Aidan could only nod his thoughts still in chaos. What were they supposed to do now? Now that even the police was unwilling to help, he was at a loss of what to do. And the police might be right. There was nothing he could do. He could only wait. Wait for a phone call. A phone call which would give him the news of his beloved. And only time will tell whether the news were good or bad.

CHAPTER TWO: THE RUNAWAY BRIDE

She was running. Even if her heels were broken, her head was bleeding and her tears were blinding her, she was still running like mad. Even if her lips were parched, her throat dry and her feet aching, she was still running. She could not stop.

Except she did not know her destination. She only knew that her instincts were screaming at her to run as fast as she could. It was as if her life was in danger. Like someone was after her. So she ran till she felt her legs could no longer carry her and she finally fell to the ground on her knees gasping desperately for oxygen.

What the hell was happening? She was still in a state of shock and she felt even more horrified as she looked down at herself and saw that she was wearing a white dress which had been torn and was pretty much in shreds. As she looked more closely, she suddenly guessed that it was a bridal attire. It was her wedding day? Who was she running from then? The groom?

But wait a minute. Who was the groom? Or more important; who was she?!! Hell, she could not even remember her own name. She had no memories of what had happened to her and why she was in such a state.

It was not a simple matter of heart; of that she was damned sure. She could have been running because of a heartbreak or a small lover's quarrel. Her heart was speeding as if it was in some danger and she was feeling someone after her. But she could not remember her own name; how could she remember the one who was trying to harm her?

As she squinted her eyes to remember, she felt such an excruciating pain in her head that she had to grab it with both hands to block away the pain. And then she felt her hands getting wet and with apprehension she looked at them only to see them filled with something red. Was that blood? Was all that blood hers?

But there was blood everywhere. On her dress which no longer looked white. It was brown, red and grey. She could not help feeling that all that blood was not hers. Feeling for her head again, she winced in pain and felt the source of where the blood was coming from.

She must have fallen and hit her head while she had been running and must be suffering from temporary amnesia. That was the reason why she could not remember anything. Everything would come back to her in a while. But for the time being, she had to get a grip of herself as she was getting impolite stares from the passersby and she stood up quickly.

Hell, she must be looking quite a sight. With her hair falling out of place from her coiffure and her torn dress. Thankfully, it did not even looked like a wedding dress anymore. It looked like somebody had ripped off the bottom part. Maybe herself. To be able to run faster.

She knew where she was. Manhattan. Near the "Theodore Roosevelt" park. Amazed at how well she knew this region, she felt sure that she lived nearby. And felt even more frustrated by the fact that she could remember the place she was but nothing about her own life.

But she could hardly ask anyone if they knew her. Not when her attacker was still after her. Or had she been hallucinating about that as well? For she was running in her wedding dress. There must have been something related to the wedding or something which had happened between herself and the groom for her to run like that.

By the look of it, she was sure that her life was in danger. Was he trying to kill her? For what reasons? Money most probably. Was she rich? How come she had not seen anything out of her scam of husband? She must have been pretty stupid. Or stupidly in love.

Wrinkling her nose in distaste at the kind of woman she could have been, she stopped walking as her legs were aching and sat on a bench just outside the park. When she again tried to remember who she was, she got another headache so profound that this time she had to grip the sides of the bench to brace herself from the pain. It was unbearable; as if her memory had subconsciously blocked out whatever trauma she had been through. It must have been pretty intense. And the suspense was killing her.

Casting her speculative thoughts aside, she decided to take things into control. It would lead her nowhere thinking about what had happened because the more she thought about it, the more her head was pounding. It was time she took thing in her hand. First of all, she had to change into some decent clothes but she had no money with her. Feeling for any jewelry, she found that she was wearing a small chain with a gem heart pendant. It could be gold and diamond for all she knew. She had to be very careful while selling it in case she might be tricked.

As she removed the piece of jewelry from her neck, she looked at it closely and felt a pang at the thought of separating from it. It felt as if she had been wearing it for a long time since it was precious to her. Had someone gifted it to her? Maybe her so-called groom.

Then how come she was not even wearing an engagement ring? From the mark on her middle left finger, it was there but she no longer had it. Maybe she had flung it on her fiancé's face before breaking off the marriage. Everything was hinting that the culprit was the groom but it was hardly surprising. She could remember no one else and had only assumed there was a groom because of her wedding dress. She could be deadly wrong also.

Looking around her, she found a store and went to inquire about the price of the jewel. Thankfully, it looked a nice shop and the elderly man was impressed after examining the chain.

"This is a nice piece of jewelry you got here my lady. Where have you stolen it from?' he asked staring at her disheveled state. And she could hardly blame him for his skepticism. Hell, she was also starting to doubt her character.

"I was wearing it. Listen, I have lost my way. Can you please give me some cash and I'll be on my way," she replied in an arrogant tone which made the jeweler look twice at her. She knew what he was thinking. From her voice, she sounded sophisticated and like someone who was used to command.

And everything about her was making her speculate on what type of person she was. Was she a spoilt brat? Or maybe some rich heiress whom someone had been trying to kill for the money. But that didn't explain her wearing a wedding dress. It looked nothing like a wedding dress now. And she looked nothing like a rich spoil heiress. More like Cinderella.

Finally, the man gave her four hundred dollars; a price undervalued she knew but beggars could not be choosers, right? And that was the way she was feeling right now. Like a bloody beggar. Thanking the man graciously, she left the store and headed for another to get a decent piece of cloth.

Her taste in clothing she discovered was classy but four hundred dollars were everything she had and she could not afford to be outrageous. So she bought the cheapest pair of jeans she could find; something she could wear again and again. Along with two black top and a white t-shirt. Trying to be minimal in her expenses, she bought a pair of flat sandals and felt odd knowing instinctively that she was used to high heels.

When she was properly dressed, she went for a meal in a nearby store and bought a bottle of water to last for the day. Now all she had to do was to arrange for somewhere to sleep. By tomorrow, her memories would be back and she could even go home.

She was tired and all she wanted to do was lie die and rest before hitting the road again and find something which would lead her to her past life. But it was a luxury she could not afford as it would be night soon and she had to find a shelter.

After walking for several miles asking for directions, she finally landed up in a convent. As she walked inside, she felt weird as she was not even sure whether she was a believer or not. She could not remember anything about herself but she knew where to find food or clothes. What kind of illness was that?

She had not enough memories about amnesia but she knew that it was a very improbable disease and she could get her memory anytime. But whenever she tried to jog her memory back, she felt that excruciating pain and had given up. She feared she might aggravate her case.

Not wanting to face anyone yet, she marched towards the church and was thankfully unseen. It was peaceful inside the church and as she knelt down to pray, the words came naturally in her mind and she sent a fervent prayer to God. At least she was a Christian. She felt relieved to discover things about herself that was not too negative.

"My dear child," she heard someone called to her when she had finished her prayers and she whirled round in fear her heart beating like it would get out of her chest.

"Father," she whispered her initial fear subsided. She could ask for refuge in the church for the time being as when she had asked for a stay in a hotel they had told her it was hundred dollars and she could not afford to spend so much for only one night. She had nothing left to sell and she would have to take up some work soon for her survival. So she had to save the maximum.

"Can I stay here for the night?" she asked deciding to trust the pious man. It was not as if she had any choice but she was staying on her guards. It was what her instincts was telling her.

"What happened to you?" Father asked seeming to pick her trouble expression. "Have you had any problems at home?" he asked her gently.

And she decided to be frank with him, Shaking her head, she explained.

"No, I...I don't remember anything. All I know is that I was r...running from someone who was trying to hurt me...me," she stammered as fear settled in her heart again and try as she might, she could not shake the feeling of cold that came over her.

"Oh, I'm sorry to hear that. You don't remember your name?" he asked her with a frown and asked her to sit on one of the benches.

When they were both seated, she told him whatever she recalled. And how she had survived till here. Thankfully, the father seemed to believe her story. And was ready to offer her a sanctuary at least for the time being. She did not have the audacity to ask him for how long; she had to go with the flow.

"Stay here for the time being. I'm Father Christopher. I will call for Mother Katherine and Sister Margaret," he told her and she was left alone with her thoughts.

The names mentioned by Father Christopher had rang a bell in her head but she was too tired to think of anything else. And besides she was not even sure which name it was which reminded her of something.

It was already late and all she wanted was to rest her tired mind. Tomorrow was going to be another day, she convinced herself. Who knows maybe she would get back her memories or at least part of her past and she would find out her identity.

"Oh you poor thing," cooed a female voice and she turned round to be greeted by two bug women who looked at her like she was some lost puppy. "I am Mother Katherine," the one who seemed eldest introduced herself and she felt another pang at the mention of the name.

Katherine. Did it mean something to her? But before she had time to ponder over the matter. The other woman advanced her extended hands to her introducing herself as Sister Margaret. They looked nice and she smiled back for their benefit.

"I'm.. sorry. I don't even know my name," she said and Mother Katherine winked at her.

"That's not a problem, love. We will call you Mary until you find your real name. Now, come with us. We will show you around."

Kate was happy to oblige and thanked Father Christopher profusely before heading for the convent rooms.

"We have a local doctor but he comes only on Sunday mornings and we had to wait for another week for his consultation," Mother Katherine was saying and she nodded in guise of appreciation. It was more than she could have asked for. "We could call him over so that he could examine you though.

"Oh no, thank you for that. I feel a lot better already and I don't want to burden you with my presence. I am grateful for this shelter. And I'm willing to get some work done in some guise of payment," she told them and they both tusked in unison.

"Oh, I insist," she quickly put in when Sister Margaret opened her mouth to protest and refuse her proposition more probably. "I hate being idle so I'd better make myself useful around," she assured him.

"Fine. But this is God's home. No one has to work to stay here. Come let's arrange for your room," he said.

It was nothing fancy. It was a small room filled with dirt as no one had used it for some time as the two women told her. But she was thankful for having a shelter to sleep and had no time to mourn about her life. She was no whimpering female who would complain at the first challenge life threw her way.

No, she was made of sterner stuff than that and she was glad of who she was turning into. It was a nice feeling discovering herself and liking her personality. She was proud of the woman she had turned out into and she believed that all the credit went to her parents who must have done a wonderful job with her.

Thanking the two women one again, she placed down her bags and decided to postpone the arrangement of the room for the next day. She hated disorder, she realized but it was too late to start cleaning up the room. She was dead tired and all she wanted to do was clean herself and get some decent sleep.

Before Mother Katherine left her, she asked if she could get a shower and was led to a small bathroom where there was no shower but a pail of water.

After having carefully washed her hair to avoid hurting herself on her wound, she wiped off herself and changed into her white t-shirt. It was long enough to cover her thighs and she had checked her room before going to the bathroom. It contained a lock and she would shut herself in the room for the nights.

It was not that she was not feeling safe. As Mother Katherine had said, she was in the house of God and had nothing to fear. But her initial fear would not fade and her instincts were telling her to be on her guard.

Sneaking back into her room, she locked herself and finally sat on the bed feeling much better. Raking a hand through her long hair, she bent her head in her hands and tried to jog her memory one more time. And along came the usual excruciating pain.

But instead of rejecting the pain like she had been doing, she welcomed it. And buckled under the force of it when her mind came up with a complete blank. She was going to give up when suddenly she had a flash of herself standing in front of a full-length mirror wearing a beautiful wedding dress. Her famous wedding dress. And she was smiling.

As quickly as it had appeared, the image was gone and when she searched her memory again, there was nothing but a blank. And her head was reeling from all the concentration. She had to stop or it will driver her crazy.

After taking some painkillers Father Christopher had given her, she rested her head against the pillow and pondered over her new discovery. She had been a happy bride. How was that possible? When her hunch was telling her that she had been running from the groom.

Well, not her hunch but every possibilities led her to believe that there might have been trouble in paradise. Maybe she had been happy for the wedding. Before discovering the truth of her fiancé most probably.

Her mind still full of those thoughts, she dozed off and suddenly she found herself in front of the mirror again; the very one she had just seen. And she could feel her heart filled with happiness. It was unmistakable the way her heart was light with bliss and she was admiring herself in front of the mirror.

When suddenly her white dress was filled with something red oozing out of her body and she looked at her reflection in shock. It was blood. Somebody had stabbed her in the back and she could do nothing about it. All she could do was stare at herself losing so much blood.

But she was not dead. She was still looking down at herself with some kind of wonder on her face. And she mouthed something. Something which sounded like "Aye" but she could not make out the whole word.

There was blood everywhere. And she heard a sadistic laughter behind her. In a daze, she could not make out whether it was male or female and when she whirled to see the person, she woke up with a start.

Beads of perspiration ran down her temple and she frantically searched for comfort but found herself alone in an unfamiliar room.

Out of pure reflex, she wanted to scream but felt like someone had stuffed cotton in her mouth. And she was trembling like a leaf. Like somebody wanted to kill her.

Trying not to panic, she wiped her tears and squinted her eyes to adjust to the darkness of the room. There was no one around. She was alone in a small shabby room. Sagging against the pillow in relief, she realized she just had a nightmare and remembered her misadventure and how she had landed in a convent. Calming herself down, she gripped the mattress on both her sides and tried to breathe normally.

Her heart would not stop thudding though and she replayed the nightmare in her mind over and over. Was it true or was her subconscious playing tricks on her? Had someone tried to kill her? Was that why she had run from the wedding? Or was there something else? Something more serious? Something she was refusing to see?

She tried to remember the name she had cried out during her nightmare but could not even remember the syllable. It was frustrating how one always forget the most important thing in a dream. Finally, she gave up trying to make out what happened; she had to stay strong to face whatever was waiting for her in the future. But she had to figure out what had happened before the one who was trying to hurt her found her out.

Eventually, she concluded sure that whatever had happened to her, it had something to do with blood. Whenever she closed her eyes, she could see blood everywhere. And she could even smell the foul smell at the back of her mind like it was engraved or something.

Which meant that only one thing; she must have run from something very very serious. And with that thought in mind, she rushed to the bathroom throwing up all the food which she had ate earlier.

CHAPTER THREE: THE PLOT THICKENS

Somebody screamed. Aidan felt his blood chill at the shrill ominous sound and his heart leapt in fear in his throat. Without thinking, his heart said only one word. Kate! Something had happened to her. Rushing upstairs to the west wing, he followed the repeated sounds being closely followed by Alex and Ryce.

As he barged into the room from where the sound had come from, he nearly slumped in shock at the sight in front of him. It was Jade who had screamed. And her face was grey as she stared at something on the floor in front of her. Following the direction of her gaze, he felt his breath catch in his throat and Aidan felt sure that his face was mirroring her expression.

They were both staring at a the back of a dead body which laid on the floor of the attic. The face was indiscernible as it was facing the floor with a knife stabbed in the ribs. And it was hard to make out anything as there were so much blood everywhere.

Before Aidan could anticipate it, Jade fell to the ground her body going limp. Aidan gulped unable to react as he continued to stare at the dead body in front of him. Alex who arrived at that particular moment let out a harsh expletive and Ryce also sagged in shock.

Aidan felt his body ready to give way and he had to grip the door handle so that he could still stand upright. Bile of nausea mounted in his throat and had it not been for the arrival of the other females, he would have puked the contents of his stomach right then. Taking in a deep breath, he steadied himself and tried to look strong for the sake of the ladies.

There was a foul smell in the attic and he blocked the women from entering the room. It was going to be a sight which would haunt them for the rest of their lives and he wanted to spare them that ordeal. When Alex brought Jade lifeless body out of the room, he asked Judith to tend to her daughter.

"Go. We will take care of the situation here," Aidan rasped and was thankfully backed up by Bryan Stafford, the husband of Caitlin.

"Here, give me Jade," he gracefully offered.

"Oh my God! Is she alright?" asked Judith in a small voice as he watched her son in law pick up her youngest daughter's lifeless body.

"Come, mother," Bryan said leading the ladies away from the horrible scene and thankfully they followed having missed what was going on. As soon as they were out of earshot, Aidan looked at Alex with mortification.

"Who could it be?" he asked in a trembling voice no longer caring if anybody could see him as a weak person. A great deal had happened and it would take a lesser man not to show his emotions now.

"I don't know. I don't think we should move the body or try anything. I'm calling Greg over," he said determinedly.

Aidan feeling numb could not respond and whenever he tried to look at the body to determine the owner, he felt bile rise and he had to look away. What the hell had happened? Was it the reason why Kate had fled? Had she witnessed the murder? Or had it been a suicide?

There were so many unanswered questions in his mind and time stood still as they replayed one by one in his head. He barely looked up when he heard Alex answer his phone. Who could have committed such a crime? Fear gripped his heart at the mere thought of what had happened to Kate. So his instincts had been damned right; she was in some serious danger.

Swallowing, he watched as the police arrived and blocked the area. Gregory Kyle was a well-built man who took charge of the situation immediately. It suddenly became an important case and the place was surrounded by cops. Everybody was busy looking for hints and evidence; everything was happening in a flash almost like in a movie. When they had done with the inspection, they whirled round the body and Aidan froze as he discovered the identity of the victim.

Edward Bigfoot. It was Edward Bigfoot who was lying dead in a pool of blood and everybody was raw with shock at the discovery. Edward Bigfoot was dead!!! The statement rung in his head until his mind drew a blank repeating that sentence over and over like a mantra.

Who could have killed him? And for what purpose? Edward had become quite friendly with them after the break up and Aidan had admired him for having taken everything sportively. Of course he had still acted snobbish sometimes but they had never bothered since they knew that ultimately he was a kind soul. And now that he was dead, the mystery was getting more complicated.

"How come nobody saw the body before?" Gregory was asking Alex and the latter shrugged in response.

"We have all been worried. And everyone was gathered in the fitting room trying to understand what had actually happened. We had no idea that there was a dead body in the attic. That is not until Jade found it."

"Where is she?" queried the inspector. "I need to ask her a few questions."

"She has passed out at the sight of the dead body. Bryan has called a doctor to look after her and I think she is feeling better now. But we have not moved anything from the room and I would appreciate if you don't trouble her for the time being."

Gregory Kyle nodded and Aidan could not quite figure out whether it was in agreement or understanding. Then he frowned in concentration. "Why were you worried? There was a wedding in the house, right?"

"Yes but my eldest daughter has gone missing only one hour before the wedding ceremony," informed Alex with a voice which spoke volume about his state of mind.

"Kate has disappeared? But why didn't you call the police to signal the disappearance of your daughter?" the superintendent asked sounding surprised and Alex told him how the cops had reacted when they had come over for investigations.

And the superintendent was really angry with his subordinates' behavior and promised to take severe actions against them. They should have at least searched the house, he informed them. And they would have found the dead body.

Aidan felt glad that at least they would be reprimanded and would not behave so coldly with another family in distress. However, the next sentence of the policeman drove him almost mad with worry.

"This is unfortunately a murder case; not suicide as the victim has been stabbed thrice in the ribs and if he had attempted to kill himself, he would have stopped after one attempt. How were you related to him?"

And Alex told him the truth; that he was the son of his wife's friend Abigail Bigfoot and had been engaged to his eldest daughter Kate one year ago. But Kate had never been in love with him and had broken the wedding some weeks before.

Gregory frowned. "Well it's not looking very good for you Alex. Your daughter has gone missing and she is the only one who knows what really happened. For the time being, we are going to seize the castle for further investigations."

"What?!!" asked Alex frowning at his friend. "What for?"

"In guise of evidence. We will have to search the house for any evidence and the castle is quite big so it will take some time. You can contact your lawyer if you want; we don't have much choice," replied Gregory looking apologetic.

Aidan knew he was only doing his job and it was after all a case of murder. His blood froze at the mere word and he cringed to imagine what could have happened to Kate. With his future wife missing, it made everything even more complicated. Damn!

"Okay," agreed Alex grumpily. "We will shift to our penthouse for as long as necessary."

"Alex?" called Gregory when all three men of the house was going to find their wives to inform them of the unexpected relocation. "There's more," he simply said and Aidan instantly knew it was going to be very very bad news.

Hell! As if things were not bad enough. Bracing himself for the incoming blow, he immediately felt a hand on his left shoulder as if offering support. Before turning, he knew it was Ryce who had also anticipated the bad news and was providing his help.

"As Kate is missing, she is the prime suspect for the murder,' Gregpry delivered in a dead tone and each one stared at him incredulously.

What the hell did he meant? That Kate had killed Bigfoot? Why the hell would she do that? It made no sense; Kate was not a murderer! Hell, she would think twice before even killing a damned mosquito.

"Greg..." started Alex and stopped his sentence midway when his friend lifted a hand in his direction.

"You don't need to justify yourself. I'm not saying that she is the culprit but until another clue has been found, we...," he faltered as Bryan joined them and Alex turned behind to see who had just arrived.

"It's okay," Alex gruffly said. "He's part of the family."

Gregory must have remembered that Bryan was the son-in-law because he nodded immediately and went on. "Like I was saying, until we find a concrete proof, Kate is the prime suspect. And the fact that Mr. Bigfoot was the ex-fiancé is not helping at all."

"What is that supposed to mean?" asked Bryan angrily.

Aidan could hardly utter a word as shock had taken control over his mind. The insinuations of the police officer were deep and he knew that Gregory Kyle would not be lying to them. So, he reigned in whatever protests his heart was making in order to better assimilate what was happening. What was the point anyway? Kate was missing and even if she was suspected as the murderer, the police could not arrest her.

"Well, the main scenario is that Bigfoot had tried something rash with your daughter to avenge himself and she had tried to defend herself. And has unpremeditatedly stabbed him to protect herself."

"But Edward was very friendly with us even if the marriage was cancelled. He never held a grudge and Kate had reimbursed him every penny he had spent for the ceremony," Aidan was quick to offer as information.

Gregory shrugged. "I could also be completely wrong. Or maybe Bigfoot had been acting all that time and waiting for the appropriate moment to avenge his humiliation," observed the police officer shrewdly and Aidan was baffled.

Was that possible? Was it possible for someone to behave normally when he had so much hatred in his heart? Aidan was no longer sure about what had happened anymore. It was like an intrigue and the more they tried to think about it, the more possibilities were coming up. But he was not ready to accept that Kate was a killer. Not even in self-defense.

"But what is not making sense in that theory is where did she get a knife during the heated argument?" he speculated ready to defend his love until he had no concrete proof.

"Exactly!" defended Alex who seemed unwilling to believe that his daughter was the culprit. "And Kate would not hurt anyone. She cannot be a murderer no matter how petty I sound," he protested and his friend patted his back.

"I know how it feels. I will try my best to find out what happened. Don't worry. For the time being, I've sent my squad looking for her at every hospitals or the nearby terminals. I will give you a report before the end of the day," he consoled the suddenly tired looking father.

Hospitals? Damn how could they have overseen that fact? Of course she might be wounded and had landed in some hospital for treatment. Aidan mentally slapped himself for not thinking about that possibility.

"And let's hope that Kate gets back home soon," Gregory added and Aidan read his double meaning. It meant that if Kate had only run because she was afraid of what had happened, she would be back soon. But if she stayed away for too long, it meant that their theory was well-founded. That she was the killer.

Hell! What a mess! Was he right? Had Edward tried anything before the ceremony and Kate had defended herself. But why would Kate kill him? It did not make any sense. She could have cried out for help. But maybe she had and no one had heard her because they had been busy with the wedding preparations. And she had been left with no other choice.

But to kill? That was presumptuous. Why would she kill him if he had made advances towards her? Had he tried to rape her? Rage surged through him instantly at the mere thought but he kept his temper in check as there were other more important things to deal with.

"Please let us know as soon as you find out anything," intervened Bryan seeing that his father-in-law was getting depressed. "Here, take my card," he offered the officer his business card and the latter dutifully took it.

"Couldn't someone else have barged into the house for robbery or something?" asked Ryce speaking for the first time since the dead body has been discovered.

Gregory nodded in answer to his question. "We have not eliminated that possibility. It could also be that Kate had nothing to do with the murder and has been kidnapped. But we have to get a ransom call before being able to move forward with this case. For the time being, Kate is considered as the prime suspect since her ex fiancé was killed."

"I'm sorry. It's hard to accept that Kate could have killed somebody. And Aidan had said, where would she find a knife if ever Bigfoot had been trying to rape her or something?" Ryce mused and even the officer seemed to agree.

"You're right. But if she is not the culprit, she will try to contact someone soon," he said looking in Aidan's directions. "She might ask for help and explain what had actually happened. Please inform us if you find anything," he implied and Aidan nodded his head in acquiescence.

Gregory was not the enemy here; he was trying to help. And if Kate was terrified of someone, she would contact him for sure. For he knew Kate trusted him more than she trusted herself. Then he pondered over the fact that the police officer had emphasized on the words "if she is not the culprit".

Which meant that otherwise, she would stay away from home because she might be incriminated. And Aidan found himself wishing that he would have some news of her soon. It was not that he was doubting Kate; he was damned sure that she had not committed the murder. But if it meant absolving her from any crime, it would be better if she came back. As soon as possible.

Things happened in a trance after that. The police blocked the west wing and nobody was allowed in. They were asked to leave the premises the next day and Alex cooperated without any further ado. Gregory was a good man, he would help them as much as he could.

Caitlin was very affected by the turn of the events and they had to call in the doctor to look after her. Judith was trying to take the news with a courageous affront and whatever doubt Aidan had in her regard had disappeared. Judith Thornton was a pain in the ass but not someone vile. He could vouch for that fact with his life.

Jen and Jude were shell shocked and were trying to be strong for everyone else since they could not afford to break down. As for Jade, Aidan discovered that she had regained consciousness and had her color back in her face. But she was still trembling and nervous whenever approached. The doctor had prescribed her some pills to calm down her nerves. His mother was hysterical and beyond consolation.

"Oh Aidan!" she cried while everybody was trying to talk at the same time with the latest news being fed to them by Alex. "How could this happen?" she moaned and Aidan consoled her.

"Don't worry, mom. We'll find her, I promise. Wherever she is, I promise I will find her out and take care of her."

"I hope so. I can't imagine in what state she must be," whispered Judith in a stricken voice and Alex hugged her immediately. And Aidan felt a void in his heart at the couple in front of him. How he missed feeling his beloved Kate's arms around him. How he missed her lovely face. How he missed her smile and sultry looks.

Sighing, he closed his eyes to block the vision and hugged his mother instead who wiped her tears and promptly hugged him back.

"I cannot believe that the police is suspecting Kate," added Caitlin in a small voice. "I mean everybody knows how kind-hearted she was," she said lifting her eyes to her husband for some support.

The latter nodded to her and explained that it was only an assumption due to lack of evidence. The police had not confirmed anything yet and would eventually get back to them. And they did. Faster than he had imagined.

Late in the afternoon when everybody was busy packing, Gregory phoned to announce that they had found a wounded girl in a hospital and wanted them to come over to identify her. Apparently, the victim was badly hurt and her face could hardly be recognized.

Everybody tensed at the news and Alex asked the women to stay back and they would go to the police station to identify the body. But Caitlin was adamant; she wanted to come along and Alex finally gave in. Fear gripped Aidan as he imagined Kate looking swollen and hurt but he was also relieved that she was still alive and prayed that it was her.

Please please God. His heart in jeopardy, they drove to the hospital and he was almost unwilling to enter the room. Feeling butterflies in his stomach, he slowed down his steps and wished Ryce had come along with him. Since Caitlin had insisted to come, her husband had come with her and Ryce had stayed at the house to look after the others.

Nobody was safe yet. There was still the possibility that a gangster was involved in the turn of events and he must be waiting to strike anytime. It was better to be safe than sorry.

As Alex and Bryan preceded him in the hospital room, he strained his ears to listen to whatever they were saying. Finally, he caught on some words about the victim being in an accident and could not stall the suspense any longer. Taking a deep breath, he entered the room and cringed at the sight in front of him.

The girl was unconscious and had her face completely damaged. But as Aidan tried desperately to search for any similarity between the face in front of him and the one etched in his mind, his heart sank with acute disappointment.

It was not Kate. His Kate could be doing much worse…

CHAPTER FOUR: STAYING ALIVE

Mary was getting used to her new life. And her new name. She was surrounded by wonderful people who were taking great care of her and in return, she cooked for them. She was a great cook, she discovered. And she enjoyed cooking for everyone in the convent.

She was also good with accounts and therefore helped them with the budgeting and saving for the future. It was something she was used to do she was sure since she seemed to focus on every detail and derived astute strategies to maintain their current possessions.

Maybe it had something to do with her profession. She must be a banker or involved in a similar lucrative business that required such kind of creativity. She grimaced at the thought finding that particular profession quite mercenary something which she was not liking. But she had no right to be prejudiced especially in the state she was.

Two days had passed since her sudden rebirth and she had still not remembered anything yet. And except for the quick memory which she had on the first day, nothing had flashed again. It was futile trying to remember as ever time she would end up with her unbearable headache and she had no choice than to give up.

Thankfully, the wound on her head no longer ached and was on the verge of healing. She was having some difficulty in combing her hair but the sisters were always willing to help her. It had taken her little time to integrate among them.

During her free time, she had been given access to the library where they had a vintage computer but she had googled about the disease "amnesia". From what she had learnt, there were several types and she assumed that hers was followed due to the trauma she had been through. And having longer periods of amnesia would only worsen her case.

And there was no specific remedy; she had to wait for her memory to come back. There was the possibility of her to attend therapy but she had to consult a doctor for that and she was not willing to make surface for the time being.

What if someone had tracked down every nearby hospital and was just waiting for her to resurface to attack again? She did not even know if there was anybody to protect her out there and it was too great a risk to take. What if she was an orphan who had only her fiancé to rely on and she had realized too late that he was not who he had seemed to be. It had to be big for her to take such a drastic step.

And when Mother Katherine had asked her to put up an advertisement about her disappearance, all she had done was stall for some time not willing to share her past with them yet. Seeing her reluctance they had not pressed her and she had been grateful for that. She could not afford to let her guards down so soon. It was better to be on the safe side for the time being.

"Mary?" she heard someone call her and she stopped to look at the person trying not to show her grimace at the name. It was not her name, she was sure of that. It sounded strange to her and she so wanted to be called by her name.

"Yes," she answered Sister Julie; a lovely lady whom she had grown close during the two days of her journey.

"Mother Katherine is calling for you," she was informed. "I think she had called for the doctor and would like you to consult him for your head injury."

Trying not to panic at her words, Mary smiled submissively not wanting to show her emotions to the woman. But how could she consult a doctor? And why had Mother Katherine taken such a step without consulting her? There would be enumerable questions about her past and they would try to persuade her to come out in the open.

And how would she be able to convince them of something she herself was not sure? How to convince them that somebody was attacking her when she had no proof whatsoever of what had happened? The doctor would only blame it on her imagination and she would be helpless as she had no concrete proof of what her six sense was telling her.

Damn she was so screwed!

Sighing, she slowly went in the direction of Mother Katherine's office and knocked politely on the door. She would talk to the doctor, she decided. And told him the truth. If he insisted, then she would have to take extreme measures.

"Mother?" she asked opening the door and looking inside to find an elderly man sitting opposite Mother Katherine. They had been in deep conversation and stopped immediately at the sight of her hovering at the door. Instinctively, she knew they had been talking about her and groaned inwardly at the unexpected turn of event.

And just when she had thought the drama was over and she would settle down. And focus on getting her memories back rather than trying to save her skin.

"Ah Mary. Please come in," Mother Katherine gestured her to come in at the same time as she spoke. "Here, meet Dr. Carl. I called him earlier so that he could get a look at the nasty wound on your head."

Reluctantly, Mary entered the room and greeted the doctor politely. It was like she felt apprehensive and suddenly she knew the reason why. She was not willing to learn the truth of what had happened to her. It was something her mind had blocked and whatever it had been, it was not something she would like to be reminded of.

Her thoughts instantly went to the groom who must have betrayed her and that was why she had not expected that blow. Was she going to be able to remember her past? What was she going to do if ever she found out that her future husband had been trying to assassinate her? Would it break her heart once again?

Was she still in love with him? Would she be able to forgive for whatever he had done to her? Or she would have to give him the benefit of the doubt since she was not even sure that he was the one who had tried to hurt her.

"So Miss Mary," the doctor started as soon as she sat next to him. "Mother Katherine here has informed me that you have no memory of your past life," he asked and Mary nodded in answer feeling her heart pick up speed as her nervousness grew.

"Well, I'll leave you to it," Mother Katherine politely interrupted and before Mary could stop her, she got up and left the room.

Damn! Now she was alone with the doctor and she was feeling even more uneasy. Would he probe in her mind and find out the truth? Swallowing, she fidgeted with her fingers and tried to calm her erratic heartbeats.

"That's right. The last thing I remember is that I had been running. I don't even remember falling down and all I knew was that blood was oozing out from me somewhere," she finally confessed in a small voice when the doctor was patiently waiting for her answer.

He nodded when she spoke and she felt her unease gradually fade. It was going to be alright. She was going to remember everything and the doctor was going to help her.

"When I felt my head, I realize that I must have fallen down while running," she continued.

"Let me see that wound," he asked in the same gentle tone and Mary bent her head to show him where she had been hurt.

"Does it hurt?" he asked feeling the wound gently with his fingers and Mary tried not to wince at the pain she felt.

"Not like before. But when I accidently touch it, I can still feel some pain."

"That's normal," the doctor informed her. "The wound has not dried up yet and it's nothing serious. But I think it's the thing which had triggered your amnesia."

So it was amnesia. Her heart sank as she heard the doctor pronounce the word. She had been hoping that he might have diagnosed it as concussion or something. Something milder than amnesia. Even if she knew all along that it was amnesia. Wishful thinking on her part, she knew. But she was grasping at the tiniest thought of hope for the time being to keep her sanity.

"And Mary is not your real name?"

"No, I was given that name the first time I came here. I don't even remember my own name," she whispered hating the way her voice wavered at the thought. It was depressing that she had no idea who she was.

To have no memory of her past life was a horrible thing and she desperately to feel something. For the past days, it was as if something had been switched off in her and she was only surviving. Oh, how she wanted to live again.

"I understand the feeling," the doctor consoled her but she doubted it. "It must be difficult. Something really traumatic must have happened to you and your mind has subconsciously blocked any memory. Have you tried to remember anything at all from your past?"

And Mary nodded. "But every time I concentrate, I have this terrible headache which becomes unbearable and I have to stop."

"Okay. That is normal. Your mind is not ready for the memories yet. And have you remembered anything? Anything at all?"

Without thinking, she nodded again and said. "Yes, I remembered myself in my wedding dress and smiling happily. I have that flash on my first night here and cannot remember anything after that," and could have bitten her tongue after the words were out.

"Wedding dress?" he repeated stunned. "You were getting married?"

Shrugging, she tried to catch up on her gaffe. "Well, it looked like a wedding dress but I could be mistaken. In fact, I'm sure I must have imagined the whole thing. I am so tensed these days that I see everything the way I want to see it," she even tried a laugh to mask her distress.

The doctor seemed skeptical when he nodded this time and Kate gulped down her worry. Damn! What had she done? She should be more careful when she opened her mouth next time.

"Have you contacted the police?" was the next question and Mary cringed despite having anticipated such a question.

"No," she croaked uncertain of what she would say next. She felt the familiar constriction of her throat every time she thought of someone finding her out and she gasped for air. The doctor quickly placed a glass of water in her direction and tried to soothe her back.

"Now, now. Don't panic. It must have been something really traumatic as you are not willing to remember what happened to you. That is why you are having headaches every time you try to go into your past," Dr. Carl observed pushing back his spectacles on the rim of his nose.

Mary felt her burst of panic recede hoping that the doctor would not force her to go to the police. She did not understand why she was so reticent because going to the police might mean that she would eventually get all the help she needed.

But what if she did not remember the person she was supposed to be afraid of? What if he got to her before she had time to discover his real identity? With her memory loss, it was difficult for anyone to help her, even the police.

"I.. I.. have the feeling that someone is trying to kill me. Or that my life is in danger. That's why I'm unwilling to come out in the open. With my memory gone, I don't even know who to trust or who to beware of. I need some time," she pleaded desperately.

Thankfully, the doctor did not press the matter.

"Well, I'm giving you some painkillers for the headache. But I would still advise you to report your case in a police station. Your family must be dead worried about you now. If something had happened, you must have left without any note and they would be thinking the worst," he suggested gently and Mary could see his point.

But every time she thought about turning to the police, she felt a premonition that something even worse would happen to her. And the doctor explained that it was part of the disease. The thing she had blocked was not ready to resurface yet.

"Maybe time is what you need," he mused. "But don't take too long as your case might aggravate if you stay too long from your usual surroundings."

"What do you mean?" she asked puzzled.

"Well, if you were surrounded by familiar things, it would help you remember your past more quickly. Something might trigger your memory but the more you stay away from what you are used to, the more difficult it will be for you to remember."

Of course. That was what she had read on the net last night. That having longer periods of amnesia would only worsen her case. That was what it had meant.

"I will take your leave then," he finally said and Mary was relieved that he was understanding her situation. It was going to be fine; her sanctuary was still safe for the time being. Smiling feebly, she saw the doctor out and went to thank Mother Katherine. Even if she had done something Mary did not appreciate, she had done what she had thought was best for her and Mary could not hold a grudge against her.

But even Mother Katherine after hearing what the doctor had to say was asking her to contact the police and Mary felt insecure. Were they going to turn her in? So she decided to tell them the whole story just to ensure that they were on her side.

"I'm afraid something terrible might have happened to me and I'm still in danger. I don't even remember who was my attacker but my instincts are clear. All I know is that I can feel somebody after me," she confessed brokenly.

"But what about your family love? They must be worried sick about your whereabouts," Mother Katherine said in a soothing voice seeing that Mary was depressed.

"I know! But what if my attacker gets to me before my family? I will be unable to defend myself. I must have been damned lucky to have escaped the last time."

"Oh dear! This is so complicated. I never thought stories like that happened in real life too. It's more like we're in a novel or something," said Sister Margaret.

Mary could not help agreeing to that fact. She had never known that amnesia could be so dramatic. And the fact that she was lost was not helping at all. If she had her family around her, maybe she would have gotten part of it back. Or feel better.

"I feel so sorry for you my child. We understand what you're going through. And we swear that we will protect you with our lives," Mother Katherine told her and Mary felt a warm glow around her heart. Religious people were so beautiful.

"Thank you Mother. It means so much to me," she replied her voice cracking with emotions. "I'd better go to my room and rest," she said. Her famous headache was back and she wanted to lie down and forget her worries. And pretend that she was part of the convent like she had been doing for the past two days.

As she administered herself with another painkiller, she laid down on her pillow wincing with pain as her head pounded mercilessly. It was like somebody was playing drums inside her mind. Would it never stop?

Massaging her head slightly, she tried not to think about the questions hovering in her head. The more she thought about them, the more confused she became. And the harder it was for her to go on. But it was not helping; the pounding would not stop.

Trying to ignore the pounding, she closed her eyes and tried to relax her mind by thinking about the seaside. It was relaxing to imagine waves crashing around rocks and the peaceful swaying of the water.

Even at nights I can't rest... Is this some sort of a test?

That thought suddenly peeped in her mind and she opened her eyes in shock. Hell, where had that come from? Why was she having such thoughts? It was a beautiful sentence but she had no idea from where it had surfaced.

Was it part of a poem? It fitted her situation anyway and whoever had written it must have been talented. She cast the thought aside trying not to make a big deal out of it. It must have been something she had read somewhere. And it had flashed in her mind but the question was that why she remembered a damned poem but not her own damned name?

She was trying not to curse especially when she was in such a sacred place but she was getting frustrated. Her talk with the doctor had exhausted her when all she wanted to do was block her memory from coming back. She wanted to start a new life never going back where she knew would hurt her beyond words.

As her eyes drifted close again, she relaxed as her mind pictured her peaceful scenario once again. But suddenly when she was least expecting it, she found herself walking down the beach wearing a white dress. Her damned wedding dress. It was a picture which would not leave her mind and even in her dreams she could see that the dress was torn.

Which meant that the picture was stuck in her subconscious and she could still not figure out the whole dress even in her dream. Then she found herself staring at her reflection in the famous mirror and she could picture it in more detail this time. She was looking like a happy bride once again with her hair carefully done and her make up impeccable. And she was smiling at her reflection grinning like a fool. A fool in love.

It was going to be the best day of her life. It was the way she was feeling. When suddenly the whole nightmare started again. She felt her dress going red and found the pointed part of a knife piercing through her ribs. The image was clearer now. There were things her subconscious could better grasp in this second nightmare.

Stunned, she felt for the red thing coming out of her body and discovered with horror that it was blood. But she was still standing in front on the mirror like last time. She had not collapsed to the floor even when the knife pierced through her. Wasn't she supposed to be dead? And the weirdest thing was that she was not even feeling the pain. Her mind was processing those facts even in her dreams, that was how disturbed she was.

And as she looked up at her reflection in the mirror, she saw her lips move. She was calling out a name. And this time she could figure out the name she had been trying to say. Aidan. Numb with shock, she could only stare at her reflection whispering the name over and over again like some mantra.

Was she warning herself against her attacker?

Then once again, she heard the sadistic laughter behind her and like last time, she tried to whirl round to see the face so that she could associate the name with it. But this time she did not get the chance to turn around. She felt an excruciating pain in her head and suddenly there was complete blackout.

CHAPTER FIVE: SILVER LININGS

It was already a week. A week since the day he had been supposed to become the happiest man on this planet. And now he was the complete opposite. The saddest person on earth since he had no news of his love.

No phone call for ransom. No news of Kate in hospitals or even at the airport. Nobody had seen her running in her wedding dress. Nothing. It was damn frustrating and he felt helpless because there was nothing he could do.

The police had concluded that Kate was on the run and they were looking for her everywhere. They had asked a photo of her to print and placed the "WANTED" logo beneath and Aidan could not help feeling how ridiculous it was.

Instead of finding information about the real culprit, they were wasting their time accusing Kate as the murderer. He was losing his patience and had decided that the police was up to no use. They were too procedural in their mission and would never find Kate out.

That was why he had called Ryce and Jennifer to meet him at a restaurant somewhere outside Central Park. They had to discuss their next steps and he was damned sure that his two best friends would help him find his beloved. Even in the worst time, Ryce had been always ready to support him and Jennifer was strong enough to leverage the two of them.

"Ryce! You came," he said frowning as his friend arrived at the restaurant alone.

"Yeah of course. Sorry about being late. Flint is not well and I asked Jen to go back to Brooklyn. She was crying like a whale but I managed to convince her for the sake of Flint. I also succeeded in extending my holidays for another month to be with you."

Aidan sighed his relief. It was what he needed. Thankfully he had been on holidays himself as it was supposed to be his honeymoon time. Ironic, wasn't it? He and Kate had a long way to go. They had waited ten years for their love to materialize only to end in such a dramatic way.

"Do you also believe she's running away from me?" he asked without beating around the bush as soon as they had taken their respective seats. He had to know what Ryce thought. He did not care about what the others thought of him. But Ryce mattered. Ryce Vin Connor was his brother.

"Are you kidding? Of course not!" he proclaimed and Aidan felt immense relief seep in as his shoulders sag. It felt like a weight had been lifted off him. So he was not delusional. Kate could not run from him. She had loved him since forever and more than he could ever have imagined.

And he had loved her back. But he had always known that he could never match the love Kate had for him. It had been unconditional, pure and simply out of this world. Something he had not deserved. Maybe that was why his love was missing. Maybe it was a way for God to punish him for his past mistakes.

When he had been in university, he had estranged his friends and had turned into a harsh man due to some misunderstanding. And his colossal ego had not helped at all. Therefore he had crushed anyone who had ever come across his path. Was that why he was getting punished today? Because he had been ruthless in the past? But if it meant making him someone who deserved the love of Kate, he was willing to go through that hell.

That was how much he loved her, he now realized. Kate had always been around and he had taken her for granted. But not anymore. If she came back in his life, he would treasure every moment he spent with her. Not if she came back. When she came back.

"Thank you for that. I needed to hear the truth from you," he finally said and Ryce shrugged as if it was a great deal.

"Man, she loved you like mad. There's no way she could have run away from you. I am damned sure of that fact. But what astounds me is that what could have happened? I mean she has not been kidnapped and must be on the run, right?"

Aidan sighed. It was what he been raking his head about. Where the hell could she be? "I really don't know. But frankly speaking, I have not ruled out the option that she might have been kidnapped yet."

Ryce frowned at him. "Really? What about the fact that we haven't received any ransom calls yet?" queried his friend rationally.

"Who knows? Maybe somebody is keeping a tab on the castle and has found the place surrounded by cops. I mean who would take the risk of calling the place in such a case? And I'm feeling sure that somebody has kidnapped her for revenge."

He heard the sharp intake of breath as he voiced out his inner feelings. He had let one week go by intentionally so that he might have a clear head about the situation. He refused to believe that Kate had ran.

Even if something terrible had happened, she would have contacted him by now.

"If she had run away for whatever reason, she would have contacted me by now," he explained his theory to Ryce who nodded in understanding.

"Yes she trusts you more than anything. She would have found a way to call you," Ryce agreed quickly and Aidan found solace with his words. He was so glad Ryce was on the same wavelength as he was.

But there was not a single clue about what had happened except that Edward had been stabbed with a kitchen knife.

"I am damned sure she must have been kidnapped. She must be in a deeper fix than we are envisaging. The problem is that we have no smallest clue about what happened. I wish that we could at least get a hint about her whereabouts. That is why I'm so sure that she had been kidnapped. But who could have kidnapped her?" he reflected.

"And the police are not helping. Now that Kate had not shown up, they are sure that she had committed the murder. Even with everybody vouching for the fact that Kate could not be a killer," sighed Ryce.

"Tell me about it," muttered Aidan ruefully removing a small notebook from his pocket. "I have given up any hope about being helped by the police. Here," he said handing him the notebook after having opened a page. "I have made a list of my potential business enemies. I think we should start searching from here."

Ryce seemed to scan the names and made a grimace. "This is a hell of a list," he finally observed handing him back the notebook and Aidan felt his heart sink with disappointment. He had thought that Ryce would be the one who would help him in his search if not anyone else.

But he had been wrong. Even Ryce was feeling like he was overdoing it but he was simply unable to sit back and relax until something came along. It was too much to ask of him. He was sure that Kate needed him and his heart was restless all the time.

"Don't get me wrong! I will help you without any second thought. But you have more than twenty names written on that notebook and how the hell are you going to trace those people down? And even if we do you should not forget that they are affluent persons and some of them might not even live in the States."

It was rational what he was saying. But his heart would not listen to whatever reason his friend was trying to make him see.

He had to find Kate.

"And besides even if we manage to track them down, how are you going to make sure that they have Kate? It would take us months if not years for this mission."

"I was thinking of hiring investigators to keep an eye on each one of them but you're right. It would take a long time. But what if we never have any news of her? What if nobody calls for a ransom? If only you knew how sitting and doing nothing is killing me."

Ryce patted him on the back. "I know the feeling. Trust me. Sometimes I hate myself for being so powerless. But it's the only choice we have," Ryce reasoned and Aidan knew he was not the only one worried about Kate. Ryce considered her as his sister and he must be missing her too.

Aidan sighed. Everything was complicated. Even the Thorntons and Bigfoots relationship had strained about the death of Edward Bigfoot. Which was predictable in a way. Not that Aunt Abigail was blaming Kate for her son's death. No, she thought too highly of Kate to even think that she might be responsible for such a crime. But she had lost her only son and Aidan could understand the state she was in.

When Abigail Bigfoot had received the news of his son's death in the afternoon, she had stormed in the castle followed by her daughter Nathalie who looked aggrieved too. The timing had sucked because it had been just before they had their things ready to move to the penthouse.

"I want to know what happened," she asked the cops brusquely and was shocked to learn that his son had been murdered.

"What do you mean murdered?" asked Nathalie addressing the cops and not even looking in their direction. She was holding her mother close as the latter had been too shocked to make the merest response.

Nathalie Bigfoot was the bold and beautiful sister of Edward Bigfoot, not to forget mercenary. She had been interested in Aidan before he had started dating Kate. But Aidan had only been using her to find out about Kate's real feelings for him. And it had worked to the perfection.

Kate had been damned jealous of the attention he had paid to Nathalie and Aidan had got what he wanted without even bothering to clarify things between them. But he had not seemed it necessary to give any explanations because it had not been as if they had dated or anything; he had only accompanied her to a few shopping trips.

But when Nathalie had found out about his relationship with Kate, she had been furious and had not talked to any of them since. Especially after having discovered that Aidan was worth billions, she had regretted letting go of that opportunity ever since.

"I'm sorry miss. Your brother is dead," an unfamiliar policeman informed them wearing a sad expression. It was not unusual for them not to recognize the police around; there were so many in the place that Aidan had difficulty keeping pace with each of them.

"Who?" croaked Aunt Abby sagging against her daughter and Aidan guessed that she was asking about the killer.

"We don't know anything yet, ma'am. We will give you some more information as soon as possible. The investigation are on and the body had been taken to the hospital for further analysis. We're sorry for your loss."

Both Abigail and Nathalie were crying and when Judith made a move to comfort them, Nathalie raised a hand to stop her. She was seething with rage.

"Don't!" she rasped angrily. "It's all your damned fault You have been playing with Edward for a long time now!"

Judith had let out a painful moan. "Don't say that, please. I've lost my daughter too," Judith had pleaded to her best friend but the latter had been too immersed in her own grief and had refused to answer.

"Don't even dare come to the funeral," added Nathalie nastily and dragged her mother towards the car.

And that was how they had not even been allowed to attend the funeral of Edward. It had been hard and the whole family had mourned his death but they had preferred avoiding any scandal. But that was one week ago and the Bigfoot had still not allowed any of the family around their house ever since, not even to offer their condolences.

"I know but I'm quite desperate," Aidan replied returning back to the present focusing on his more urgent problem.

"Don't worry mate. I totally understand your situation. Hell, I cannot imagine in what state I would be in if it had been Jen instead."

Ryce loved Jennifer as much as Aidan loved Kate. They had all four been best friends at the same university and it was thanks to the couple that Aidan had been able to realize how much he had loved Kate.

"Yeah and the hardest part is not knowing."

Ryce sighed in answer. There was nothing left to say. Aidan raked a hand through his hair and pinched his nose in concentration. Ryce had rejected his plan of action which left them back to square one. And he was not ready to just sit and wait for the kidnappers to contact him. It was too damn risky.

But he had no other choice. Even if his theory about the kidnapping was true, he had no clue where to start looking. It would kill him if he had to wait for another week; if he had to go through another week without her.

He was missing her like hell. Especially during the nights where she used to warm his bed. After the six months of only waiting and waiting, their reunion had been explosive and Aidan was still basking in the aftermath. Kate was one woman who blew off his mind with her innocence and sexiness and he wanted to have her forever in his life.

Forever, he sneered to himself. And got another pat on the back at his expression. Picking up his courage, he tried to smile at Ryce and got up.

"Well, I'm on my way to the police station. Go back to the castle and look after the family," Aidan told him and giving him a friendly hug. Even if his trips to the police station were not very fruitful, he could not give up on Kate. Not now, not ever.

"Sure," said Ryce returning the hug and heading towards the truck they had borrowed from Alex. Aidan was not ready to go back yet as he wanted to roam around the streets with the hope of finding someone who would give him a clue about what had happened on his wedding day. Something which he had been doing for the past week.

There must be someone who had seen something. Putting a hand in his pocket, he looked around as he walked and asking some people if they had seen the picture of Kate. As expected, most of the people around were eying him warily and giving him negative responses.

Just when he was about to give up, he met a small boy near Theodore Roosevelt park who vowed that he had seen her. His heart picked up speed at the unexpected twist. Kate had been here? It meant that she had not been kidnapped. Damn!

Kneeling down, he showed the little boy the photo more closely. "Are you sure it was her?" he asked finding it difficult to breathe around his constricted heart. Damn he so wished God would not be so cruel as to give hope before deflating his heart again.

"Yes. She was sitting on that bench and crying. She looked dirty," the boy named Dwight told him. "I wanted to ask her what was wrong but she looked so sad," and Aidan was surprised at the maturity the six or so years old boy was showing.

Aidan was first relieved to know that Kate was alive and in good health. But the fact that she had been sad was gnawing at him. It was clear now that something had happened to her. There was no way that she had run from the wedding, he was sure it concerned the murder of Edward. Maybe she had witnessed the murder and had no other choice than to save her life.

But that did not explain her one week of silence. And Aidan felt something terrible grip his heart. Why was it so complicated? She must not have gone too far. He was outside Central Park and he had never ventured so far since he had never really believed that Kate had run.

It had been easier for him to believe that Kate had been kidnapped. Because Kate had trusted him so much. And he wanted to know what had happened to that trust. She could have at least phoned him!

Picking out a bundle of notes from his purse, he handed it over to the boy as reward and moved away his mind still filled with questions. He was moving away when he felt something or somebody stopping him by grabbing his shirt.

"There's more."

Aidan was shocked and berated himself for being so stupid. It was the first silver lining he had gotten after a whole week and instead of probing for more questions, he was falling in his 'poor me' mode. He had to get a grip.

"Yes tell me," he asked gently after swallowing twice to ease the tension past his throat.

"The lady cried for a very long time. And then finally she went there," he said and Aidan followed the direction of his finger. Dwight was showing him a nearby jewelry store.

Puzzled, he frowned thinking why Kate would go to a jewelry store. It did not make sense. But he decided to keep his inner thoughts to himself and focus on the trail he had gotten after so much difficulty.

"And?"

"And I don't know. I saw her entering that jewelry store and I had to go back home. I never saw her after that," and Aidan nodded.

"Okay, stay right here, will you? I'm going to inquire in the shop. I might have some questions after that."

The boy nodded and pocketed the money while Aidan made his way to the store. Filled with anticipation, he felt sure that Kate had found refuge in the store and when he pushed open the door, he felt disappointed to find an elderly man alone in the shop.

"How can I help you sir?" the man asked and Aidan immediately showed him the picture of Kate he was always carrying in his purse.

"Have you seen this woman? About one week ago?"

Aidan watched as the man frowned at the picture for several seconds and he tried hard to hang in to the suspense without letting his impatience get the better of him. The suspense was killing him. Finally, the man pushed his thick glasses on his nose and shook his head in a negative answer. Aidan felt his heart sink.

Hell, how was that possible? The little boy must have been mistaken after all. It had not been his Kate. His Katie would never have left him.

And just when he was about to leave the store, he froze as he caught sight of it. It was lying in the show piece window and there was no way he could not recognize that damned chain. The necklace he had gifted to Kate on her nineteenth birthday.

CHAPTER SIX: JUST MISSED YOU

Someone was looking for her. Someone called Aidan. Her blood froze as she got the news from Sister Julie and she had to grasp the nearby chair for support. So it had not been just a hunch; there was someone called Aidan in her life.

She had remembered the name as soon as she had woken up from her nightmare on the third night and the nightmare had repeated ever since. She could focus on more details each time. Like she had been crying when she had felt that knife pierced her ribs. And the name Aidan had always been in every dream.

Which meant that he had to be linked to what had happened and to why she had ran. But who was Aidan? Was he the groom or the murderer? Or was he the groom murderer? Why would she call out the name Aidan if he had nothing to do with her being murdered?

The message in the dream was clear; her life was threatened. That was why her instincts had told her to run. It was pretty clear to her and she could not make anyone understand her plight. And he had to be pretty desperate to track her down till here. Not to mention dangerous.

And Mary was sure that the man wanted to harm her. Wouldn't he have come with the police if he was clean? From what she had heard, he was alone and was carrying a picture of her and asking if anyone had seen her. Hell, how smart was that damned murderer? She had not set foot out of the convent ever since she had come here and nobody had come to visit since the doctor.

"Please sister. Not a word," Mary signaled the sister frantically from afar. She so wanted to get a glimpse of him and she was told that he was in Mother Katherine's study. Stealthily, she tiptoed outside the study and peeped into the room to get a look of the man. To her disappointment, he was standing with his back to her and she could not make out his face.

But he was nothing like she had imagined. From where he stood, he looked lean and almost perfect. Gulping down her unease, she felt her heart pick up speed and rapidly hid behind the door to listen to whatever he was saying.

"Are you sure you haven't met this woman?" he was asking and his voice reflected some worry. At the sound of his voice, Mary felt her head started to pound again. Her subconscious knew this voice and was trying to warn her against him.

"Could you please try again? I have another photo of her. Maybe you could have a better look. Please," he almost pleaded when Mother Katherine shook her head.

"I'm sorry but I cannot help you sir," was repeating Mother Katherine and Mary knew how difficult it was for her to answer him without lying. The mother superior was after all a woman of virtues and she could not lie, not even for a good cause.

"Her name is Katherine too. She has been missing for a week now. We have been worried sick and...." he seemed to falter and Mary processed the information in her head. So she was named Katherine. No wonder she had felt a pang every time they had used the name Katherine around her in the early days.

"How are you related to her?" asked the Mother and she felt her heart pound in anticipation at the question. She would finally get to know who he was and decide whether to confide in him or run from him.

"Kate and I were engaged to be married," he said and Kate felt shock ripple through her. She had been hoping that he would not turn out to be her evil groom but it seemed that destiny was against her. "She ran on our wedding day but I know she has not run from me," he delivered in a confident voice. "She loved me so much."

Kate sagged against the door as she heard the latest confession. She was starting to have mixed feelings. He sounded sincere like someone who had suffered a lot and she could not make up her mind if he was acting or not. Not from the other end of the door. Maybe if she had seen his facial expression, it would have been easier to gauge his emotions.

"I'm sorry to hear that, son. But I'm sure that wherever she is, she would eventually hear your plea," Mother Katherine said loud enough for her to hear and Kate knew that she had spotted her outside the door.

"I certainly hope so. But I really don't know what to make of it. I was so sure she had been kidnapped. Until this morning. When I met a boy in a park who had spotted her. I cannot believe she is running from me. Something must have happened to her," the beautiful voice sounded again and Kate wanted to reach out and comfort him.

What was wrong with her? Why was she getting carried away towards a complete stranger. And suddenly she understood how she had gotten herself in such a fix in the first place. Damn she must have been thinking with her hormones instead of her mind. No wonder that man could fool her so easily.

"She trusted me more than she trusted herself. I still cannot understand who she is running from. And why she had not contacted me yet," he added and Kate who had decided to move back to her room retreated her steps back. Was she being completely mistaken about the whole thing? She could be completely wrong about what had actually happened. But it was too big a risk for her to take.

Hell, she had no memory whatsoever of her past life and one could hardly blame her if she was being cautious. She did not want anyone to take advantage of her situation and if her life was in danger she had better tread carefully.

"She will. Maybe sooner than you expect."

"What do you mean by that?" he asked and Kate felt an alarm trigger in her head. Had he doubted anything. The answers he was getting were cryptic and had a double meaning but if Aidan could decipher them, it could only mean that he had a sharp mind.

"Keep faith my son. I will pray to God that she gets back to you soon."

"It's hard not knowing if she's fine or not," he finally delivered after a few minutes of silence and Kate felt his pain through his voice. Why was it so hard for her to trust him? Why was it so hard for her to trust anyone? It would seem that her amnesia has not only taken her memories but has also altered her faculty of trusting. But maybe she had always been that dubious.

Still indecisive about what to do, Kate tiptoed back to the corridor while she watched the man thank Mother Katherine profusely and made for the door. As he turned, Kate had to mentally remind herself to breathe. She had never expected him to be so... so handsome.

His lean well-toned tall body was the perfect fit for her tall figure and his ebony hair was neatly swept back from his face. Kate felt an unexplainable urge to run her fingers through them and could have kicked herself for her over aging hormones. But once she got a look at him, she was mesmerized and could not look away.

When he smiled at Mother Katherine at the door of the study, Kate noticed lines of worry round his mouth and the smile did not quite reach his eyes. He had a three days stubble on which gave him the look of a dangerous mouthwatering pirate.

Mouthwatering? Now where had that thought come from? Was she losing her rational as well? He was breathtakingly beautiful for a male and she found herself wishing fervently that he was not the one who was supposedly causing her harm.

Her eyes were riveted to his face like a magnet to metal. As she stared at him from the corridor, she was glad he could not see her. Even from a distance, she was breathless watching the way the lines played on his face or the way his muscles rippled.

"Well, thank you for your time Mother. I will take your leave now. And here's my card. Do call me if you get to know anything," he said and Kate was so busy admiring him that she had no time to react. She felt her heart stop when suddenly he looked in her direction.

Her whole body went rigid and it was a torture trying not to make the slightest movement. Her heart was pounding so loud that she feared he might hear it. But there was no way he could see her. The corridor was dark and her body was almost behind a door.

As he squinted his eyes, Kate gulped at the beauty of the two specters. They were dark green. Like a dense forest. God was so unfair sometimes. Why did the eyes had to be outstanding too along with everything else?

Finally, he shook his head and made his way to the exit door and Kate let out a long repressed breath. However the relief was short lived as she watched his retreating back from the window and felt like her heart was breaking into millions of pieces.

What the hell was wrong with her? She had to make up her mind once and for all. Okay she was attracted to him but it was plausible since she had been ready to marry that man. But not when she had found out that he was a damned murdered?

How could her head overrule her mind? What kind of person did that make her? Well, she was glad not to have been in front of him. If she was having such reactions on just spying on him, she could hardly imagine what it would be like facing him. Wrinkling her nose, she watched him stride off until he was out of sight and heaved a huge sigh of relief.

"Oh no, you don't!" sounded behind her which made her jump guiltily. It was Mother Katherine who wore a severe expression.

Oh-oh. It wasn't looking good.

"I don't know what you mean," she prevaricated.

"You are the Katherine he was looking for. I cannot believe you are hiding from your past. And from him. He seemed really worried about your disappearance."

Kate flashed guiltily at the words. "But I'm sure he has been trying to kill me. And you know about the nightmares. Why would I call out the name Aidan if not to warn myself against the murdered? And why else would I run from my own damned wedding?"

"Don't swear!" admonished the Mother superior instantly. "You're in a convent! The fact that you are avoiding him does not make any sense. If he was the killer, you should have at least confronted him about it. I don't think he would have killed you in front of all of us!"

She had a point. But Kate did not know why she was feeling so apprehensive. The doctor had warned her that her present ailment was preventing her from getting back to her old ways because she was still not ready to confront her past. It was a weird feeling; one she could not even explain.

But Mother Katherine was right. That man could hardly kill her in front of so many people and she should have asked him what had happened after she had run from the wedding. But she had a feeling she did not want to know.

Hell, how was it supposed to be when your bride has left you at the alter? It was downright humiliating and not to mention painful. She was behaving like a fool.

"And if he had the intention of killing you, he wouldn't have come in the open asking about you in the first place. He would have followed you or something," Mother Katherine added and Kate felt even more guilty at the implied accusation.

She was practically being accused of overreacting but she could not explain her sixth sense. It was telling her that someone was after her life. And whatever anybody said, it was not making any difference to her. But after seeing him, she felt different. Like she was missing out on something important.

Kate sighed as she had nothing to say. The Mother superior was more keen to side up with that stranger than her. And true to her words, the latter thrust a business card forcefully in her direction and she moved back out of pure reflex.

"Here, call him. Don't go alone if you don't want to but at least talk to him."

And when she took the card, she read his full name. Aidan Flint Waldorf. Out of their own will ,her fingers stretched against the name and she found herself caressing it. And she felt a sense of déjà vu. She was damned sure she had done this before but she could not place any event to it. Damn her memory loss!

"Who knows maybe you have been calling out the name to save you," Mother Katherine said wisely before leaving her and she stood transfixed. Was she right?

As she went to her room, the words echoed in her head and she finally accepted that it was a possibility. Something her frenzied mind had not taken into consideration because she was in her survival mode. Maybe Aidan was not the attacker but her savior. Maybe she had been over dramatizing the whole story and she had only freaked out from her wedding.

Despite herself, she found her heart accepting this option and she felt a shudder of anticipation at the thought formed in her mind. Maybe he had not betrayed her as she had been imagining. Maybe there was a hope for her and her fiancé after all.

And there was only way to find out. She would call him tomorrow. There was no use hiding from her past anymore. Come morning, she would ask Sister Julie to accompany her and if she did not get back after two hours, Mother Katherine would call the police.

It was the only thing she could do. It was time for her to face the past. As the evening went by, she become more determined and decided to ask Sister Julie to make the call tomorrow. She would not expose herself to any danger at first. If he was the murderer, he would jump at the first occasion offered to him and he would waste no time in killing her.

As she shared her idea with Sister Julie, the latter appeared more enthusiastic than her. Hell, everybody seemed to be under his spell.

"Oh, Mary. I mean Katherine. I'm glad that you have finally decided to meet him. Talk to him and listen to whatever he has to say," replied Sister Julie.

"You can call me Kate. Katherine is so like the Mother superior," she said and they both laughed at her joke but she could feel her insides clench with worry. Or was it anticipation? She could feel herself looking forward to meeting that man Aidan again.

"Do you think we must take a man along?" she queried pursing her lips in worry as she tried to figure out a way. But there was no male in the convent except Father Christopher and Dr. Carl.

"I think it's a good idea. If you will feel safer. There's Kent who lives near and he usually helps us with the cleaning during the winter. I will ask Mother Katherine if he can accompany us. And don't worry he's well-built and would be able to defend you if need be. Except that I don't think it will be necessary. That boy is too pretty to mean any harm."

Did she have to add that last part?

"Right, see you in the morning then," she bade Sister Julie goodnight and moved to her room her mind still in havoc.

How would she react if she found out that he had been trying to kill her? It would break her heart once again no doubt but it was time for her to face her fears. And besides, she might find out about her family or there must be other people worried about her.

Staying at the convent was a temporary reprieve and she could not settle in her sanctuary forever. It would make her a coward. And she was sure she was worth more than that. With those thoughts in mind, she settled against her pillow after her usual night bath preparing herself for another nightmare session.

It was a normal thing for her to have nightmares those days and every time she woke up, she would feel her hair damp and her whole body shaking terribly. But it would seemed that every time she prepared to go to bed, she was mentally rehearsing the nightmare also. And it came naturally.

It was the same nightmare which replayed in her mind however and try as she might she could never go further than the sadistic laughter. It seemed too real to blame it on her subconscious and she had been clinging to her nightmares to derive her conclusions.

But no more. Tomorrow was another day and she would finally get answers to her many questions. It had been one week of going crazy about not knowing anything about herself and it was more than she could take.

Suddenly, just as she was trying to doze off, she heard a sound and jumped on the bed looking around fearfully. It was a sound of someone who had landed on the ground and she felt her heart pick up speed. Who could it be at such a late hour? It must be past midnight and by the past week she had spent in the convent, she knew that everybody went to sleep early.

Was someone trying to break inside to get her? Or was it Aidan who had seen her even in the dark and had waited till the night to attack her? She was being paranoid and she felt sure that her amnesiac mind was conjuring such frightful images to scare off.

Sitting up in bed, she tried to calm herself down as adrenaline kicked as her overactive mind was assessing option after option. As she got down from her bed, she squinted in her dark room to see if there was someone around. But it was so dark that she could not see anything, not even when her eyes adjusted to the lack of light. With trembling fingers, she switched on her bed lamp and to her uttermost relief found no one hovering in her room.

It must have been a figment of her imagination. But she was damn sure that she had heard a sound. It could have been some cat who had entered the convent. She was still debating whether to look for it or not and strained her ears for any other sound.

The silence screamed back at her and she berated herself for her exaggerated foolishness and sagged against her pillow again. Switching off the light, she found her position and closed her eyes to sleep. And instead of having pictures of her in her wedding dress, she found herself fantasizing about some handsome man with green eyes.

This was no flashback. Even in her present state, she was drooling over the man like some foolish teenager. How was that possible? What kind of woman did that make her? Was she promiscuous? Sleep eluded her and as she closed her mind from the image of Aidan, she heard another sound in the corridor and jumped off the bed again.

There was no way a cat could collide with the chandelier in the corridor! Trying not to panic, she switched on the light again and got up to check whether she had locked her door.

Before she could reach the door, she saw the knob turn and her flight instincts took over. Whirling round, she frantically looked at the window making up her mind whether she could jump or not. When she felt a hand over her mouth and her cry came out as a muffled sound.

Instinctively, she struggled against the hand and found herself back in her nightmare but this time it felt more real.

CHAPTER SEVEN: DOWN MEMORY LANE

Aidan felt his heart literally stop as Kate struggled against him in a state of turmoil. It looked as if she was no longer with him and was fighting something over which he had no power. But he knew if he removed his hand, she would scream the place down and he would no longer be able to confront her. Relaxing his hold against her mouth, he caressed her to soothe away whatever was taking over her mind.

"Hushhhhh sweetheart, it's me. Husssh," he cajoled until her body ceased to tremble and she relaxed against his body. Desperately, he inhaled her scent and felt like a drug addict after he had been deprived after a week.

Hell he had missed her so much. And when he had visited the convent, he had been sure that Kate had been hiding in that dark corner of the corridor. But could not confirm whether it was his imagination or she was real.

That was why he had decided to stay in the neighborhood to clear his doubt. And imagine his surprise when he had spotted her hovering near a window just before dusk. While he had not understood why she had felt the need to hide from him, he had assumed that maybe she was protecting him by keeping away. Whatever the reason, it was not good enough for him and he had to find her out. One week without her was all the punishment he could take.

So he had waited until it was pitch dark and it had been the longest wait of his life. When finally he had decided it was time for him to make a move, he had broken into the room where she had been. But instead of finding himself in her room, he landed with a thud in the bathroom and his dilemma had increased. How to search for her in such a dark place without getting caught?

While he had tiptoed in the dark, he had collided with something and had no other choice than to get in the nearest room. Thankfully, he had found the door unlocked and to his uttermost relief he finally saw Kate. But she had not even been looking in his direction and when she panicked, he had to find a way to stop her. Without thinking, he had muffled her cry by placing his hand over her mouth.

However, he had not been expecting her to freak out in such a way. She had reacted like someone was attacking her. And he had instantly relaxed his grasp and tried to calm her down. Now, as he held her against his body, he felt the exact moment when her fear subsided and she realized that she was in his arms. Except that instead of greeting him like he was expecting, she kicked him from behind and struggled free of his hold.

"Ouuuchh!! Kate! What the hell?" he grounded huskily clutching his ribs as he felt the pain upsurge him. And then she spoke. In an ice cold voice he could hardly recognize.

"Who are you?"

Stunned, he looked up at her still holding his rib no longer paining but he was too surprised to make the slightest movement. Was she kidding him? How could she not recognize him?!! He was the one she loved damn it!

"You don't know me?" he asked astounded and felt a greater pain when she shook her head than he had felt when she had kicked him. What was going on? It had to be his Kate. She looked the same, she felt the same. Hell, she even smelled the same. Then how the hell could she refuse to recognize him?

"I..I'm sorry. I have no memory of my past," she stammered looking at him with the so familiar golden eyes but which reflected so much uncertainty. She could not be faking it. Why would she lie to him?

And suddenly everything started making sense. Why she had not contacted him when she had run away. Why she had been hiding from him when he had found her. It was simply because she could not even remember who he was. What he meant to her. Hell!

Sitting on a nearby chair to absorb the shock of the recent revelation, he raked a hand through his hand and watched as Kate fidgeted with her fingers. It was like his worst nightmare was coming true. The love of his life was standing in front of him treating him like a complete stranger. It was breaking his heart but he knew she was not at fault.

It would seem that his punishment was not over yet. But at least she was alive in front of him. And safe. Even if she was not perfect, he vowed to himself that he would mend her.

"I'm sorry to have scared you like that," he finally uttered clearing his throat when he found his voice husky. "I knew you were here when I came in earlier. I could smell you. I know it sounds weird but the old Kate would have understood," and could have kicked himself for his gaffe.

He watched as her eyes turned sad and she looked down at her hand again instead of looking in his eyes. It was as if she was having a problem trusting him or letting him see what was in her eyes. He gulped. It was going to be hard but he would work to gain back her trust.

"I shouldn't have said that. But it's difficult for me too. How have you been?" he asked in a gentler tone and watched as she stole a quick glance in his direction. It was clear that she had not been expecting that question. Hell, who did she think he was? A tyrant?

"Ahh.. okay. Except for the bump in my head which still hurt but not as before," she said hesitantly and Aidan hated the way they were acting.

"Let me see," he said and she flinched at his words. Damn! She wouldn't even let him touch her? Not moving a muscle, he waited for her to come near him so that he could feel the wound but she remained where she stood. He still waited but when she did not budge, Aidan finally understood that she was not ready to let him near.

Damn! It was so frustrating. His Kate would have jumped in his arms as soon as he had asked for that. She had been so in love with him; so in contrast with the woman standing in front of him unwilling to even meet him in the eyes.

He sighed. "Okay, forget it. How did you get that bump?" he asked frowning suddenly in worry. Was it the reason of her memory loss?

She shrugged. "I don't remember. All I know is that I have been running and when I stopped, I felt blood all over me. I found myself in a park and tried to find my way around. But I had no memory at all. My head was pounding and I could not even remember my name," her voice broke at the last word and Aidan longed to take her in his arms. But he had a feeling she might not appreciate such a gesture from him.

He could understand her plight. How hard must it be for her not to remember even her name. Not to remember who she was or who was her family. But there was something else. Like she had been traumatized or something. And he suspected that it had something to do with the murder of Edward Bigfoot.

"When you came in earlier, it was only then that I got to know that my name is Katherine," she delivered in a small tone.

Aidan nodded but he still could not digest the fact that she was not remembering her own name. How difficult could that be?

"Your full name is Katherine Iris Thornton daughter of Alex Thornton and Judith Thornton. You have three sisters Caitlin, June and Jade. Caitlin is your favourite sister and the other two are twins," he said and watched her expression change. She became less wary as he spoke of her family which seemed to have sparked her interest.

"What am I like?" she asked in wonder and for the first time since Aidan had met her, he felt sorry for her. It was not easy to have the past wiped off from her mind and to be far from everyone who loved her.

"Wonderful," he said smiling to himself and missing the priceless expression on her face. "You're the most altruist person I've ever known; always generous and ready to put everyone else first. And so fiery," he added in a teasing note and to his relief she smiled at him. The first genuine smile he had seen from her. It was like he was bowled over.

Damn! He was such a goner. If one smile could make him drool like that, he wondered what a kiss would do. How he missed feeling her lips against his. It seemed like forever since he had taken her in his arms and make her his.

"Fiery?" she repeated and her cheeks looked suspiciously red.

"Yeah as in passionate. Especially in my arms," he answered with a wink and watched as the blush got redder.

Love making between them had been fantastic and they had never got enough of each other. It had been after seven years that they had gotten back together and the need for each other had been unstoppable. That was why Aidan had pleaded for her to marry him as soon as possible. But her family had insisted on a grand wedding and it had taken six months to finally organize the event. He should have eloped like he had wanted to do after her first marriage had been called off.

"How did we meet?" she asked him shyly and Aidan could see that she was struggling not to let him know how much she was affected.

"We have known each other for ten years now. Since university days. You were my best friend and I was too stupid to realize how much I loved you. And I let you go," he told her.

Her eyes widened at his latest confession and he felt her face go white. "I have known you for that long?" she asked not sounding too pleased at the discovery. Aidan felt sad that it displeased her. Maybe she no longer felt attracted towards him and had wanted to tell him just that. But now learning that they had been best friends, she did not want to break his heart.

Well, she was too late for that. His heart was already broken when she had not shown up for the wedding except he could hardly blame her for what she did. He was impatient to ask her what had happened exactly but he knew he had to take his time. She was the one who needed more answers than him for the time being.

"Tell me more," she said breathlessly and he was more than happy to oblige. He started from the very beginning when they were still friends and how they used to be so close that everybody believed they would finally end up together. He told her about him dating Jennifer their other best friend and how he had broken her heart. And finally how they had ended up kissing on their graduation night.

"We kissed?" she asked in wonder.

"And it was a hell of a kiss!"

"You kissed me back?" she asked puzzled and sat down on the bed as she listened carefully. At least she no longer seemed like a trapped animal and was willing to be more open with him. It was nothing like it used to be but still it was a start. And beggars could not be choosers, right?

So, he smiled back at her loving the way her eyes sparkled. "I did," he said in a self-deprecatory laugh. He was loving the way she was no longer wary and was a bit more trusting towards him.

"And then?"

"Make an educated guess," he replied looking at her pointedly.

She watched him uncomprehendingly for ten seconds and then her expression became priceless. Almost comically stunned, her hand flew to her mouth as she gasped. "You've got to be kidding me! Jennifer caught us together?"

His laugh this time was more enthusiastic as her good humor was getting to him. As always. "And there's more. Jennifer saw us and went directly in the arms of Ryce. When I ran after her, I saw them kissing in the tennis court," he grinned the memory no longer hurting him like it used to.

"Noooo!!" she shrieked and hushed herself when she realized where she was. Then she frowned. "Who the hell is Ryce?"

Aidan's grin got wider. "Ryce Vin Connor is our best friend. We have been together for the past ten years." Then he sobered. "Well not exactly."

And the rest of the story followed. He told her everything. How he had behaved after he had found his girlfriend in the arms of his best friend. How he had shunned them from his life blaming his three best friends and that had transformed him into a hard man. And finally how they got back together when she was getting married to someone else.

"I nearly lost you. Only because of my damned ego. But when we get back together after six years, I started to feel bad about the way your ex-fiancé had been treating you. And when I realized that Jennifer no longer meant anything to me. It was you all the way. And then I discovered that the reason that had made me fall in love with Jennifer all those years back was you. You wrote me the poem."

"I did? I can write?" she queried puzzled.

"Oh yes you can. The words were so beautiful that it melted my stone heart."

"Oh, then I must be a writer. I thought I was a banker or something," she mused to herself sounding confused and he was surprised at her astuteness. Even with her memory gone, she was still a smart lass.

"You are an investment officer. You work for your father in his insurance companies; it's a huge one with several branches. And you have recently inherited the enterprise on your twenty-ninth birthday," Aidan informed her biting back the question that was on his lips. He so wanted to ask her about the wedding catastrophe.

"I did? What about my sisters? Don't they get anything?" she asked frowning and apparently not liking the fact that she was the sole heiress.

"Well, you're the eldest daughter and your father could trust only you to be the successor of his empire. Caitlin is not very career oriented as she has already two cute kids to look after." He stopped when her frown deepened.

"What about my other two sisters?"

"June and Jade are studying to become doctors and they would never be able to manage the company. Alex, your father decided to give you the company and the rest of his wealth will be shared among your other sisters when he's no more."

"In that case I guess it's okay. I thought that I had stolen their share or something. Are they all okay with me inheriting the enterprise?"

"Of course. Your sisters dote on you. And it was always planned that you were going to be the successor of the company and would give something to your twin sisters in the future. They're still young and cannot manage so much money right now."

"Okay," she said finally accepting his explanations. "How did we stop the wedding?" she asked reminding him that he had not completed the story. And Aidan told her how they had to separate to finally be together. And she beamed at him.

"Oh it couldn't have been more perfect," she cooed.

"My sentiments exactly," he replied with a wink.

"It...it...must have been hard when you discovered me gone on our wedding day?" she asked hesitating at first.

Aidan immediately sobered. If only she knew! "Ahh yes. We knew nothing about what happened. We were looking for you everywhere because a running bride is hard to hide."

"Oh but I think my dress no longer looked like a wedding dress when I started to run. It was torn and dirty and even I had to look twice to realize that it was a bridal dress."

Aidan nodded. He could understand better now. And to think it had been such a puzzle only a few days back. "Yah but we didn't know that. We were expecting the worst. I assumed that you were kidnapped."

"And to think I was so near all that time," she concluded when Aidan told her where she lived. "Park Avenue. I never ventured out of the convent because I was so scared that somebody might find me. I stayed here the whole week since... since the wedding," she faltered and Aidan knew it was the right time to finally ask the question that had been burning on his lips.

"You didn't want anyone to find you?" he asked picking up on her latest confession and instantly, the new found light atmosphere vanished and her whole stance became rigid with strain. The atmosphere was so thick with tension that he could no longer breathe. Hell, even if it was the wrong question, he had to ask it.

"Why did you run away Kate?" he probed and she looked at him again frantically with her animal trapped expression.

"I...I have no idea. I don't remember," she stammered and Aidan felt that she was hiding something from him but he simply nodded.

"Is there something you would like to share with me? Anything at all that you remember from the past?"

Like why the hell you are acting so distant. Or so damned scared.

Well, of course he should not forget that there had been a murder. But that didn't explain why Kate was acting like a frightened rabbit every time he tried to approach her.

"No," she replied and instead of having anticipated that answer, he felt the disappointment consume him anyway.

Suddenly she was the closed woman again; the one who had drawn a barrier around her heart. The one who he was not at all familiar with. And he had to suppress his frustration but he could do nothing. She was not well and he must understand her. If she was not trusting, something terrible must have happened to her and which would justify the way she was behaving. All they needed was some time.

Sighing resignedly, he got up from the small chair and flexed his muscles. It was sore from his tight position and when he glanced in her direction, he caught her watching with a dazed expression. And could not help feeling elated at the discovery.

So, she was attracted to him. But was just good at hiding her feelings. He was not used to that secretive personality from Kate and was taking time to understand her. While it was hard for him and he missed his old Kate, the woman standing in front of him was elusive and mysterious and he was finding himself getting more attracted to her. Like it was possible!

"Right," he finally said when she averted her eyes again and he could not determine whether it had been his imagination or something genuine. "Do you want to wait till morning to get back home?" he asked.

And heard her surprising answer. "I cannot go back."

CHAPTER EIGHT: LOVE WITHOUT MEMORY

The moment he talked about going back, Kate felt her now familiar fears swamp her again. It was like she was in a vacuum and was sucked with anxiety. It was a feeling she was not enjoying at all but she could not help it. It was consuming her.

Because she knew that as soon as she got back at the castle, the killer would try to kill her again. She just knew it. It must be something her subconscious remembered but she knew the danger was not over yet.

On top of all that, Kate did not know what to make of Aidan. His story was romantic and if she had known him for that long, there was no way he was some gold-digger or something. And besides, if he had wanted to kill her, he would have done so by now. They were alone in a convent room with nobody as witness. That was why she had started to relax around him.

But there was also a possibility that all of it was fake. It was hard for her to start trusting Aidan again and she was still unwilling to share her nightmares with him. And in addition to that, they might just be a fluke and she did not want to feel ridiculous. At least not in front of him.

Whether she trusted him or not, the blatant attraction between them was not something she could deny. It was becoming difficult to handle as he was nothing like she had expected. During the past days, she had conjured an image of a very boring fiancé with monetary expectation from her. And she was totally unprepared to find a sexy stranger who he seemed to genuinely care for her. But it could be a ploy and it was better if she kept her guards up around him.

His sex appeal was undeniable and too flagrant to ignore. His lean body was fit and he looked like a man who loved outdoor tasks. Although he was not huge, his body was toned and Kate felt her insides melt at the sight. Even in her panic mode, she had felt the hard muscles around her and had somehow felt safe in his arms.

By now she now had a pretty good idea who would want her harm. It was her ex fiancé. It had to be him since Aidan had told her how they had broken up the marriage and everybody had found out about their romantic feelings. Edward Bigfoot must have been pretty heart-broken and had gotten back at them on her wedding day.

"How is this Edward?" she asked cautiously.

As she gazed up at him, he frowned at her with something like alarm in his eyes. "What about him? Do you remember something?"

"No," she said shaking her head vehemently not letting the fact that he was wanting her memory back get on her nerves. "But wouldn't he be the one trying to stop the wedding? How did he take the break-up?"

Aidan looked pensive and the look of alarm on his face was still present. "He took it quite well and he was pretty sportive about it. I think he finally realized that you never loved each other but was being forced by your over enthusiastic mothers," he informed her.

"All I remember is that I was running from my own wedding. And if there's no tension between the two of us, there must be someone else involved, right?"

"Yes of course. I agree with you."

"Right," she said. "And as soon as I get back, whatever had happened before might repeat itself. I mean the person might get to me and..." she stopped in her tracks not knowing what more to say and not inculcate her further.

"Is that why you're so reluctant to go back?" he asked instead of answering her. "You think someone is trying to harm you?"

She winced at his perceptiveness. She had not said anything about her nightmares yet and he was reading her mind like he was a vampire or something. How to tell him about her reluctance to go back home without confiding in him about the real danger she was feeling around her?

So, instead of replying him, she asked him another question. "What happened just before the wedding? Did we quarrel or something?"

He shook his head. "The last person who was with you was Caitlin and when she got back, you were gone. And you were the happiest bride. We couldn't wait to be married but your family insisted on a grand wedding and so we had to wait for some months."

She nodded. It was what she had seen in the mirror. She had been a happy bride. Until the last minute. The ex-fiancé must have had something evil planned and had tried to kill her on her wedding day to make a point. Hell, it even made some kind of warped sense for someone crazy; it would have been the ultimate revenge.

"Do you anything at all about my ex? Is he capable of trying or break off the wedding for revenge?" she probed. It must have been pretty hard for him to endure the humiliation of having the wedding broken because she was in love with someone else.

Aidan looked up at her and hesitated before finally saying. "Edward is a nice guy. And I don't think he had anything to do with breaking off our wedding. And besides nobody knew the real reason behind your wedding with Edward going off. We waited for six months to be together, remember? To avoid any embarrassment to the Bigfoot."

She tried for a casual shrug. "I don't know. There was blood on my wedding dress and I don't know if it was all mine or somebody else's. Do you think there is somebody in that house who would wish to harm me?" she asked stealthily deliberately using the word harm againso that Aidan would point her in that direction.

But he shook his head instead and replied. "Like I said you have a very warm and loving family and I can't see who would want you any harm. Of course you know them better than I do and with your memory gone, it's not helping at all."

At the not so subtle reminder again, she tried not to flinch. She knew it was difficult for him to deal with such a situation but if he had any idea how it felt about having one's past completely wiped off, he would restraint from passing such comments. And on top of that she had to deal with her nightmares which she wasn't even sure were real now.

Then he surprised her by saying suddenly off the beat. "Okay then let's not go back for the time being."

"You mean that?" she asked feeling hopeful.

She had thought it was going to be harder than that to convince him to stay away from the house especially since he knew nothing about her nightmares yet. For a fleeting second, she saw something in his eyes which looked akin to guilt and then as quickly as it had appeared, it was gone. And for that short-lived moment, she felt sure he was hiding something from her.

He nodded briskly. "You're not safe here as well. Let's go back to my apartment. I live in Brooklyn by the way and it's not that far from Manhattan. I prefer keep you in a place a bit far from Manhattan for the time being so that we could have a safe distance."

Safe? Safe from whom? So he knew something too and was not telling her. Hell, why was he hiding something from her? Wasn't he supposed to be telling her everything as she was already so confused? What was going on? But if he was not telling her then it must be something huge and she was better off not knowing.

Even her instincts were asking her to trust him and it was not like she had any other choice. Once that she knew he was not the murderer, she felt like she had someone to lean on and could share her worries with him. The real problem was her carnal feelings for him that she was unable to suppress. And she had to tamper down on those feelings as they were dangerous and could lead her to another level of danger.

But for the time being he was her only hope since he was the only one who could help her find her murderer. And Mother Katherine could be right; she might have been calling him to save instead of calling out the murderer. It said a lot about their relationship; she must have really loved him to call out for him even in her dreams. How she wished she could remember her past.

Glancing at the clock, she saw that it was already three in the morning and the household convent were early to rise. In one hour, almost everyone would be up and she did not want to go without saying goodbye to the only people who had been nice to her.

Aidan agreed to wait for her and as soon as Mother Katherine woke up for the usual morning prayer, Kate told her that she had to get away before anyone else caught up with her. If Aidan had found her out, then anyone else could easily track her sanctuary down.

"Oh Kate. We would miss you so much," Sister Julie said taking her hands in hers and she felt a pang of sadness leaving them behind. During her rough times, they had been her family and she had grown accustomed to the quiet life of the convent.

She tried a wobbly smile. "I'll miss you too," she addressed the small crowd which had gathered around her and hugged everybody one by one.

"Well, take good care of her son. And do come to visit us," Sister Margaret was saying with tears in her eyes.

"You never told us your full name," Mother Katherine intervened.

"It's Katherine Thornton," she answered and heard a general audible gasp.

"As in the famous Thorntons?" Sister Julie asked her hand covering her mouth in wonder.

Kate looked back at Aidan for support who smiled charmingly back at the female crowd and Kate wished that the smile was directed at her. It was so powerful and the lines around his eyes creased giving him a rugged look.

"Yes," he replied simply without giving much details and given the circumstances Kate could hardly blame him.

"No wonder!" exclaimed Mother Katherine. "Alex Thornton is a very nice man and he contributes great sum of money to our convent. I'm so glad to have been graced by the presence of his daughter who is as wonderful as the man himself," and Kate felt tears prick her eyes. How she wished she could remember her father. Everybody had a nice word about him.

Seeing her saddened state, Aidan immediately took her by the elbow and led her towards the door. "I think we should go. Our cab is here."

Aidan had left his car at the mansion and he did not want to get it since someone might suspect something. While he was away from the house, everybody would think that he was looking for her and would not question his absence. He had told her clearly of his reluctance to leave her alone under any circumstance which was comforting in a way. At least she now had someone to take care of her.

As they reached the city, Kate felt the surroundings familiar and knew that she had visited Aidan several times over. She still found it weird to remember general things but was unable to recall specific moments of her own life.

Throughout the journey, there was an uncomfortable silence which stretched between them and she was sure that he had many things to say but was holding back.

"We're here," he said as they stopped in front of a small cottage and she frowned. Was that where he lived? It was not very big but she had assumed that he was not that poor. "Don't look so fierce," he added and she jumped schooling back her expression. How come he could read her mind so well? Damn!

"It's not my house; I live in NYC. This is a small cottage which belonged to my late grandmother. I think it's safer to keep you here for the time being. Nobody knows this place. Well, except Ryce of course. We've been here several times during our university days."

Seeing his benign expression, Kate knew he was remembering the good times and she felt sad that she could not recall them too. "Have I been here before?" she asked getting down from the car and watched as he dropped a handful of notes to the driver.

He grinned but instead of answering her, he opened the door which squeaked a little before finally giving way to a beautiful living room. It was small but so homely that Kate instantly fell in love with it. Forgetting her question, she dove inside admiring the furniture and the ancient décor.

"How lovely! Your grandmother has good taste," she stated and Aidan grinned again mysteriously making her feel self-conscious.

"What?" she asked finally unable to read his enigmatic expression.

"I knew you would love it and..." he replied his grin wide and he touched her nose playfully. "...this is the exact reaction I got from you the first time you came here."

Kate smiled back at him feeling light headed. At least she had not changed and his eyes were reflecting her exact sentiments when he looked over with his green specters shining with glee. It was as if they were connecting with each other and suddenly as quick as a flash, the expression changed into awareness and pure sexual tension. It became so thick that it prevented her from moving and her heart started to pound in her chest like mad.

So powerful it was that she could not look away and she gulped down her unease as he stared at her like a feral ready to pounce on its prey. A part of her was looking forward to exploring the chemistry between them.

It must be pretty intense considering the goose bumps lining on her arms and the way her heart wanted to get out of her chest. And with just one look from him. What would a kiss between them be like? Subconsciously, she licked her lips at the thought and the forest green of his eyes became dark so dark that they were almost a sleek black.

Pinned to the spot, she waited enjoying the long wait but finally he looked away and she released a breath she had not realized she had been holding.

When he looked back at her, there was nothing in his demeanor to indicate any of the tension which had trespassed between them and she was glad. Wasn't that what the feeling in her heart was all about? Happiness? Why the hell did it feel like disappointment then?

Hell, was she crazy? How could she want to kiss him? She must be out of her mind or maybe it was the blow she had received on her head. But her every pore was aware of him and try as she might, she knew it would not go away. At least not so soon.

"Come, I'll show you your room," he said casually trying to put the awkward moment behind them and Kate followed him staring at his broad back.

Hell, even his back was sexy. Large and proportional, she wondered how it would feel to caress it and immediately berated herself for her sinful thoughts. God, what was wrong with her? It would seem that with that one look he had unleashed the pent-up desire she had been trying so hard to hide from him and it was the only thing she could think of.

She was so lost in her thoughts that she did not realize he had stopped and promptly bumped into his broad back.

"Oh sorry," she said quickly averting her eyes fearing that she might not be able to resist him if he had that fierce look around him again.

"Errm," he hesitated. "There are a few of my clothes around. You can use them if you want. You will find the common bathroom here…" and she hardly listened as he continued to give her directions to certain basic things she might need.

But she was too busy watching the way his muscles fletched with each movement and she swayed involuntarily in his direction. Unfortunately, he seemed unaware of the sexual haze she was trapped in and continued to babble about the place.

Kate wanted to shut him up with one kiss and she realized in shock that she was becoming obsessed with the man. She had to get a grip on herself before she ended up making a fool in front of him. There were more urgent matters to attend and she could not allow herself to gallivant with him around in another city.

And even if he was her intended groom, she could not give way to her carnal desires just like that. She hoped she was a better woman than giving herself to just anyone but with no memory of him, he was a complete stranger to her. She'd better keep that in mind.

Thanking him politely and almost coldly, she turned in the room and closed the door with a final click. There! That was the best thing to do. Then why did she feel the urge to open the door immediately and lose herself in his arms? The first time he had held her, she had been too panicked to enjoy the feeling of being in his arms.

Scolding herself for the foolish thoughts she was harboring, she sat down on the bed feeling nice about having a good bed. As soon as her body touched the sheets, she felt the tension of the past days take its toll on her and suddenly felt sapped of her energy.

It had been hard for her to survive without her memory and always being on guard. It was good to have his company though even if she did not remember him, she no longer felt alone. With him around, she could find herself relax knowing that he would save her.

Within no time, she felt asleep on the bed oblivious to the world still wearing her convent gown. When suddenly, her convent gown transformed into her white wedding dress and she groaned unwilling to live that nightmare again.

But it would not go away. She found herself laughing in front of the mirror again holding her bridal bouquet in one hand. Then the knife pierced through her ribs and blood oozed everywhere. Her wedding dress became stained and torn and she looked back at herself in the mirror.

Aidan save me. Aidan save me.

Then she heard the laughter again; the one which had haunted her for so many days. And this time instead of looking behind her, she concentrated on every detail. There was a lot of blood and when she turned to flee, she felt a hand on her mouth and someone trying to suffocate her.

And she screamed trying to break free but the hold was stronger and she was not able to free herself. Out of pure instincts, she kicked the person behind her and struggled frantically towards the door. Just before she ran, she turned back to look at the person she had hurt but her eyes opened in a jerk and she found herself in an unfamiliar place.

Panic overtook her and she screamed unaware that tears were flowing down her cheeks. It was like her nightmare was turning into reality. How come those unfamiliar walls surrounded her? She was so used to the grey dull looking walls of the convent. Where was she?

"Kate?" someone called and she froze as someone took her in a secure embrace and began to soothe her.

CHAPTER NINE: TABLES ARE TURNED

"Husssh. Kate, Husssh. I'm sorry baby. So sorry for having left you alone. Please don't cry," Aidan was whispering desperately in her ears as he struggled to calm her down. She was in such a desperate state that suddenly anger overtook him. Whoever had brought his Kate to this sad state would pay, he vowed to himself.

He called himself all kind of fools for having left her alone. She had seemed normal to him and so he had thought that it would be okay if he went to fetch some of her clothes from his apartment. But it had been a fatal mistake.

It had been a good decision not to tell her about murder which had occurred back at the castle, he conceded now seeing the way her body trembled. She must be terrified from what had happened and Aidan confirmed his doubt that she must have witnessed the murder of

Edward. It was the reason why he had agreed not to go back to the castle so quickly.

From what he had gathered, she knew something terrible was up and they were still unaware of the real culprit. What if he had attacked her again when she returned back? For the time being, everybody was a suspect and he could not take any risk with her life again.

While he raked his head about the possible murderer with the new found clues, he could conclude only one thing. The murderer was someone close to the family because there was no way a stranger could have gotten in the house without the help of someone to cover him.

"He's going to kill me," she uttered her voice muffled as she was pressed against his chest. "He's after me, I'm sure."

"I will keep you safe. I promise. I won't leave you ever again," he replied cooing her till the trembling of her body subsided and he felt her relax against him.

When she made a move to get up, he added a little pressure on her back to let her remain in her initial position. He was not ready to let her go yet. She resisted at first and then he felt more than heard her resigned sigh. He never knew for how long they stayed in each other's arms enjoying the feeling of their warm bodies enlaced in each other. It felt like eternity when finally she eased back and looked up at him.

Her eyes was the exact replica of a doe; looking at him warily like she was not sure whether he would hurt her or love her. Trying to convey his feelings in his eyes, he lifted his hand to brush away a tendril of hair which had fallen across her face. When he tucked it behind her ears, she whined and Aidan knew that it was not out of protest.

The golden eyes stared back at him and finally they pooled with something he had not seen for a long time. Desire. Desire for him. Something he had missed more than he had dared to admit to himself. He felt himself grow harder than he had ever been even with her and he struggled to control his urge to grab her and make senseless love to her.

At that precise moment, he would trade his soul to share some intimate moments with her but he knew it was too early to get physically involved. She had only started to trust him and he was not ready to face that cold Kate again he had met at the convent. Not ever.

With a resolution of steel, he moved away and sat on the bedside trying not to let her know how much he was suffering. It was awkward having to sit with such a hard on and he had to shift several times to find an appropriate position.

"I brought you some clothes from my apartment," he said after some time with his back to her. He knew she was looking at him with her doe eyes again; he could feel her gaze pierce his back. But he did not dare look back at her because if he found a trace of desire in her eyes, his control would snap and he would take her like an animal.

"Thank you," she whispered in a small voice. "I'm sorry for having freaked out like that. I had a nightmare," she confessed reluctantly.

"Don't apologize. What did you see?" he asked finally seeing that she was ready to open to him more.

"I...I... have been having this dream for several days now. It is the only thing I can remember. I... I don't even remember your face," she whispered in a stricken voice and Aidan felt sorry for her. But now that she trusted him, he was unwilling to interrupt her. He had to know what she had seen even if it was a mere nightmare. It could lead them to a trail or something.

So he simply waited for her to continue still sitting in his initial rigid position and not daring to look back at her.

"I...I... was wearing my wed...wedding dress. In front of the m...mirror. I was happy," she said in such a sad tone that Aidan felt his heart break. Who could have been so cruel to inflict such a wound on the Thorntons? They had no direct enemies since they were basically good people. If somebody deserved to suffer, it was him and not his sweet Katie.

"I looked happy," she rectified quickly as if doubting her own emotions and he understood her plight. She did not remember anything about herself and everything seemed to be based on guesses. It must be damned hard for her.

"W...when I find my dress stained with something red. It's b...blood. I know it's blood. There's this foul smell and it's everywhere. There's a knife stabbed in my ribs but I don't feel the pain. I look in the mirror and... and I whisper your name."

On hearing that confession, he felt surprised and could no longer resist looking at her. Her eyes were suspiciously misty and she looked at him with a new willpower.

"At first I thought I was calling the murderer's name," she said. "But now I know that I was calling out to you to save me," she added holding his eyes and telling him in a subtle way that she now trusted him. She wore such a rueful expression that at that particular moment he could not help himself falling in love with her all over again.

It was even more spectacular than it had been the first time he had realized that he was in love with her. His breath seemed to stop and all he wanted to do was hold her close. It was a pity that the tables were turned now and he could finally understand how painful one sided love was.

And Kate had loved him like that for eight years. She had fallen in love with him after their first university year but had never had the courage to confess her real feelings to him. And he had been a first class fool not to realize that the special attention she was giving him was out of love and not friendship.

Hers had been an outstanding kind of love. For the first time in his life, he felt the impact of his loss like a void in his heart. It was more painful than when his father had left him. He so wanted her to love him back amnesia or not.

And vowed that he would conquer her back even if she never gained back her memories of how much she had loved him. It did not matter if she never remembered him. He did. And he would make her fall in love with him again. If she had loved him so much once, there must be a little left within her and he would dig it out. Love was after all contagious.

Feeling positive, he whirled round to face her properly and smiled at her tenderly. "Thank you for trusting me," he simply said. Then on a more serious note, he asked. "What do you remember then? Have you seen the murderer? Anything about him?"

Kate shook her head vehemently. "No, all I know is that he had a sadistic laughter and I cannot even make out if he's male or female. Whenever I try to turn to see the face of the killer in my dreams, I have this excruciating pain in my head and everything blocks again. The doctor had warned me that I am still unwilling to remember my past and..."

"You've seen a doctor?" he queried puzzled. She had told him that she had never left the convent since she got there and had never imagined that she would have taken such a risk of consulting a doctor.

"Yes, the convent doctor. He's not a specialist but he had given me some advice. His opinion is that something terrible must have happened to me and that is why my memory blocked. My mind has subconsciously locked out the terrifying event and it also explains the headaches every time I try to remember too much."

It made sense to him. And Aidan was glad she could not remember that Edward had been killed because she would have been more traumatized by that fact. It was better to keep such a tragedy hidden from her seeing her precarious state.

"I have a doctor friend who lives close and I think we should consult him. I will try to schedule an appointment. Try to get some rest, okay," he said standing up wishing that his hard on would finally recede. It seemed that a long cold shower was due.

She looked like she wanted to say something but closed her mouth almost comically and nodded her acquiescence.

"Good. I'm going to prepare something to eat for diner then," he announced and throwing a last look in her direction, he headed for the kitchen. Then he suddenly remembered the small suitcase in his room and changed his direction. When he knocked on her door, she opened almost immediately with a question in her expression.

"I brought some of your clothes from my apartment. It would be nice to see in your own clothes for a change," he said looking down at her convent gown with distaste. Apart from being dull looking, it covered her body from head to toe and left nothing to his imagination.

"Thank you," she replied shyly. "I will join you after a shower."

Nodding, he felt happy as he started cooking for her. Something he had never done and he was starting to like the domesticated version of himself. When he had everything almost ready, he made sure Kate was still in her room and quickly dialed the mobile number of Alex Thornton.

"Son, where are you?"

"Listen, dad. I have found Kate and…" but he could get no further.

"What?!! And where are you? Why have you not brought her home yet? How is she? Can I have a word with her?"

Aidan sighed. He should have expected such an outburst. "Dad, relax. She's safe with me. She has lost her memory," he stopped and waited for Alex to assimilate the information.

"How is she coping up?" he asked after a little while and Aidan assumed that he had recovered from the shock.

"Physically, she's fine but I think she's pretty shaken up. I cannot bring her home right now. She's been having nightmares about the whole wedding fiasco. I don't think she can handle the pressure of being surrounded by the family and not to forget the murderer."

There was an ominous silence which gave Aidan a sense of premonition and he felt his hair raise when Kate's father replied. "They are still suspecting Kate to be Edward's murderer. The Bigfoot have filed a case against her and if she comes back, she will be apprehended by the police. I think it's better if you keep her away for the time being."

Aidan closed his eyes in despair. It was ridiculous! Instead of focusing on finding the real culprit, the police was wasting their time looking for more proofs which will incriminate Kate further.

"Aidan? Are you there?" asked the worried father when he did not reply.

"Yes. Yes. I'm just worried. I will take her to a doctor as soon as I get an appointment and let's just hope for the best. Have you heard of anything new?"

"No, Ryce is working close with the police and has got all the information. Which is not much. Nobody saw anything suspicious and the police scanned the whole house. They found no other finger prints or blood sample apart from Kate and Edward."

But it only meant that the killer was a clever one nothing more. He would never believe that Kate would kill someone even in anger or defense.

"That is why they're saying that Kate might have stabbed Edward to defend herself. And Edward being the ex is not helping. They're looking for her. I have talked to Greg and asked him to remove her "WANTED" picture and he had arranged for it. But she is still the main suspect and I can do nothing," said the father in a defeated voice and Aidan felt as powerless.

"Don't worry. I will come back as soon as they have anything else. If Ryce comes up with something, ask him to phone me immediately. And please don't tell anyone that Kate is with me. It might be dangerous if the killer gets to know of anything."

"I still can't believe this is happening to us. Who could have done such a demoniac act?"

Aidan sighed. It was the question of the year.

"What about the Bigfoots? How are they keeping up?" he asked suddenly remembering that Abigail had wanted to lodge a complaint against Kate a few days ago.

"Well, Abigail has calmed down but she's still not talking to Judith and I don't think our relationship would be the same again. But I don't blame them, they have lost their only son and it must be pretty tough."

"Yah," he acknowledged. That was the problem. Nobody was to be blamed about what happened and the person responsible for all that was so clever that they had no clue about him. If he got his hands on the culprit, he would make sure that he paid for all the pain he had caused both the families.

At the sound behind him, he quickly resumed the call and turned back trying not to let his worries show on his face. But it would seem that even with her memory loss, Kate was as astute as ever for she immediately asked him what was wrong.

"Nothing," he lied. "I am not able to contact the doctor. I will try later," he shrugged. "Come, let's eat."

As he turned, he saw Kate and his breath caught in his throat. She was wearing one of her old clothes; a pair of jeans which outlined her slim legs and tiny waist and a black top which showed the creamy skin just above her waistline.

Aidan found his mouth water and he stood there gulping at the delectable sight in front of him. He had almost forgotten how wonderful she looked in her usual attire. Damn! Her hair was wet from the shower and even from such a distance he could smell her. She smelled of peaches. She always smelled of peaches.

It was so overpowering that his knees buckled under the force of attraction and without knowledge he found himself closer to her. He could not resist her any longer. Out of its own will, his hand caressed her face and he tugged an imaginary tendril of hair behind her ear. He always enjoyed doing that because it gave him an excuse to touch her.

Everything faded and there was only her. Her face, her scent, her smile, her eyes. It was like he was hypnotized. And he had never felt that way for her before. It was like this new enigmatic form of her was driving him out his mind and he was feeling more attracted to her. While he missed his old Kate, this new her was like a breath of fresh air. It was a total paradox.

"Kate..."he whispered in a voice that lacked its usual tenacity and he nearly howled with joy when he felt her lean closer with her eyes closed.

She had always kissed him with her eyes before and seeing her close her eyes made him grab her in his arms and brushed his lips against hers like a mere stroke of butterfly. At the brief contact, she whimpered and he swallowed hard as he admired her to his heart content.

He did not want to scare her. Hell he himself was scared by the blatant attraction that had exploded between them after only two weeks of separation. It was like kissing a stranger but with the same taste and it was arousing the hell out of him.

Then, she opened her eyes and the golden freckles were filled with only one blatant thing. Desire. And his control snapped. Casting every rational thought aside, he plunged his tongue into her mouth loving the taste of her. When she responded back, he moaned and deepened the kiss.

It was just like old times. Her peachy scent and her sweet honey taste drugged his senses and he wanted more. It was his addiction. He could not get enough of her. Their tongues meshed and he put more pressure in her mouth like a driven man.

So engrossed was he in the feelings that he did not notice her reticence and did not realize that he was forcing himself on her. Until it was too late. Suddenly, he felt her struggling and immediately stopped cursing himself for being unable to control his desire.

He felt the well-deserved slap across his cheeks and shut his eyes in shame. How could he force himself on her like that? He had sworn to himself that he would take it slow but had failed to keep up his promise. It was not his fault that he had missed her so much that when she had melted in his arms, he had believed that his Kate was back.

But now he felt that she might never come back and he would have to live with that. Everything they had shared was only one-sided now and he could not force her to love him. How ironic was fate? Now the tables were turned. He was the one loving her while she felt nothing for him. Unrequited love was simply heart breaking and he could not help admiring her for having hold on to her feelings for so long.

He was not used to feeling that powerless and it was gnawing him. And the haunted look on her face was not helping at all.

"I'm sorry," she croaked.

He deserved it. But he was not sorry he had kissed her. If she was expecting him to apologize for stealing a kiss from his fiancée and bride-to-be, she was in for a long wait. And suddenly for the first time he felt angry for everything that had happened. All because of a b*st*rd who was too coward to even show his face. He swore that he would make him pay if he found out who had done all that. Not if.

When he found out. He would track the culprit down like an animal if need be.

"I'm not!" he replied arrogantly. "I want you."

She gasped at his boldness and looked away immediately fixing on a spot behind him. Just when he felt his heart stoop down to his heel, she answered in and oh-so little voice which made his heart leap up like in a game of hammer strike.

"I want you too," she mumbled incoherently.

It was not even a drop of what he wanted but still it was a start. She wanted him too which meant that there was hope for them. Even with her memory loss.

CHAPTER TEN: WHAT THE HELL?

Two days passed since that famous kiss episode and Aidan was avoiding her like plague. Not that she blamed him; she was never supposed to give him that slap since she had been a very much active participant in that kiss. But at some point it had become so overwhelming that she had gotten scared of the intensity of her feelings.

At first, the feelings that have engulfed her had driven her into a zone of pure passion. Something she could not remember but even in her state she knew it was not an ordinary feeling. But when he had asked for more, the heat had become too much to bear and her first reaction had been to back out.

Except that he had been too engrossed in his own throes of passion to cater for her feelings. And that was when she had panicked. And had slapped him. Not a tight slap but one to jerk him back to reality.

And it had worked. He had snapped back to reality and had released her immediately.

And she had apologized immediately because from the remorse in his eyes, she was guessing that he was blaming himself. But Kate had not been afraid of him; she had been afraid of her too intense feelings for him. But not of him. But she was too much a coward to tell him the truth.

Consequently, they were behaving like nothing had happened and had omitted to even mention the encounter. But the irresistible desire between the two of them was still obvious and unresolved. Even if they were barely talking, the sultry looks they were sending each other were enough to make her panties wet. It was that powerful.

Damn! With the attraction flaring between them, it was unable for her to focus on the problem at hand and she no longer had her nightmares. Whether it was a good or bad thing she did not know. She only knew that they were not progressing and could not hide forever.

Stealing a look at Aidan who sat opposite her on the table where they were having breakfast, she mentally debated whether she should broach the subject with him. Staying with him at the cottage was a safe cocoon but they could not hide forever. And besides her parents must be dead worried about her and from what she had heard from him, they had loved her to pieces.

Aidan seemed to be devouring his breakfast and did not even bothered to look in her direction. In some way his indifference was hurting her but she could not blame him after the way she had behaved. He had done nothing than help her and it was not his fault that his fiancée had lost her memory.

But she had not been prepared for the intense physical reaction and had reacted out of pure instincts. By the furtive glance she was throwing his way, she was mustering up her courage to ask him whether she could return back to the castle and jumped when he spoke.

"Get ready in one hour. We have to go out."

It was almost an order and she felt a rebellious streak inside her. How dared he assume that she would be ready to go out with him? Especially after the way he was treating her? Like she was not even here most of the time. Hell, she could have been a piece of furniture for all she knew!

"I was not aware of any such thing," she replied in an arrogant tone and he lifted his eyes at her with raised eyebrows.

"What do you mean?"

"I mean I'm not going anywhere with you. Not when I'm still in hiding. And especially not on a date," she rattled and could have bitten her tongue as the words were out.

What the hell was she thinking? Aidan would never try to bring her on a date. Not in her current situation. Stupid stupid stupid! Why was she behaving like some stupid love-struck fool!!

"It's not a date. I told you the other day that I was trying to get you an appointment with my friend. The doctor, remember?"

Damn! How could she forget that? She could barely focus on her problems any longer. Of course he meant the appointment with the doctor he had been ranting about for the past two days. Feeling even more stupid, she stabbed at her food wishing it was her brain and nodded in silence.

She heard his loud sigh.

"Alright, What is your problem?" he asked in a louder tone and crossing his arms like he would have with a child.

She looked back at him and calculated whether she should tell him. Then she figured what the heck. She had nothing more to lose and if he refused her advances, she would just crawl back in shame and humiliation.

"I feel like I'm part of the furniture," she stated in a voice which sounded flat even to her ears and mentally frowned at herself. Right! That is exactly the way to go if you want a man to think you're interested!

Then she realized that she had no idea how to pick up lines or to let him know that she was interested. Damn! What kind of woman that made her? A prude? Uggggh!! No wonder he was looking at her like she had grown two heads or something.

"I'm not with you," he answered still looking at her with that patient look.

"Never mind," she muttered and finished her juice in one gulp and of course choked on it. Aidan immediately came by her side and lightly tapped her back. She immediately felt the jolts of electricity on her back and moved away from his grasp.

Damn she was like a furnace ready to explode. A little distance would not hurt her right now. But when she turned to go back to her room, she felt a hand retain her from behind.

When she looked back, she saw his expression full of everything she had found two days ago and thought she would never see again. It was there! Except that he was good at controlling his feelings. For her sake, she now realized.

A warm glow feeling engulfed her heart and she felt like the luckiest woman on earth. Even in his worst moment, he still had consideration for her state and was restraining himself from coming near to her to be able to focus on their more important problem.

Time seemed to freeze as she watched his green eyes become darker with feelings and could have howled with joy at his next words.

"Trust me, you are definitely not furniture type," he said and came closer. "You're so hot that you make me want to take you here and now."

She gulped. She was already feeling liquid pool down at her core and she could not make a sound even if she tried. He was caressing her hand; the one by which he was retaining her and she felt goose bumps all down to her knees. Zillions of sensations zinged though her and she wondered if she could hold back this feeling any longer. It was so profound that she felt nothing mattered except him.

"But then…" he continued in the same light tone and lifted his other hand to lightly brush her cheek. She moaned and instinctively arched towards him for more. "… we would be late for our appointment."

Still in a daze, she understood his words only after a good three seconds. She blinked. Appointment? With doctor? Right, appointment. She blinked again. He was playing with her? The desire was still in his eyes however. Hell, he was driving her out of her mind.

Without a word, she freed herself and fled from the room fearing that she would make a fool out of herself for a second time. Damn! How could she throw herself at him like that? Even if she was attracted to him, she must be able to control herself now.

Sitting on the edge of her bed, she berated herself for being all kind of fools. He had gotten the message, she was sure. And had decided not to act on it. She did not feel humiliated but felt disappointed instead. She had so been looking forward to another heated encounter with him. She never knew she was such a wanton but she was beyond caring.

As she calmed herself down, she felt her trembling fade and she felt more normal. And decided to shower to prepare herself for dealing better with her sexual problem. Maybe she was just missing sex and it had nothing to do with Aidan.

She mocked her reflection in the mirror. Who was she kidding? It was Aidan. She had felt that damned attraction for him the second she had laid eyes on him. It was too flagrant to ignore and too dangerous to consider. Damn! She was double doomed.

After her shower, she was ready and took her time to convince herself that she did not need that kind of complication for the time being. Sleeping with Aidan would only give her regrets afterwards since she was not sure of her feelings for him.

The attraction was there but she knew nothing about him to say that she loved him or not. Loved! Whoa!! How could she think of something like that? Lust was one thing, love another. She lusted him. That was it!

And she could do nothing about it. So she decided to ignore this attraction just like he had been doing for the past two days. Two could play at such games. And besides, she was feeling a bit nervous at the prospect of meeting a doctor one again.

With this new resolution, she joined him downstairs at the end of the stairs where she found him waiting for her.

"Ready?" he asked.

And she nodded trying to mask her uneasiness. And then to her surprise, he held out his hand to her. She stood there dumbstruck and tried to decipher his intentions but he looked back at her his face impassible and she had no other choice than to hold his hand.

His large hand engulfed hers and the feelings that went through her were electric as usual. But she managed to control them this time and returned his look with a casual and neutral one. He grinned at her and her foolish heart somersaulted all resolutions flowing out of the window.

"Nervous?" he asked cockily looking so handsome that she watched him in fascination.

She shook her head and he grinned again. She was not fooling him. Not one bit.

"Come. Let's go," he said letting go of her hand only when they were seated in his black Mercedes since he had to drive.

Throughout the journey she remained silent and looked out of the window pointedly reminding herself of her two minutes ago resolution. But in spite of herself, she found herself stealing furtive glances from the side of her eyes. And noticed his firm hands. Bulging biceps. Or aquiline nose.

Thankfully, it was a short drive and the doctor attended them almost immediately. When they reached the consultation room she felt her nervousness overcome her again. And Aidan must have read her feelings because he caught her hands in his and gave a gentle squeeze.

"Okay, I need you to relax," Dr. Landon Beverly told her as soon as she was seated from what she tagged as the hot seat.

It was like an armchair and she leaned back against it feeling anything but relaxed. Anxiety gnawed at her and all she wanted to do was to get up and run. But Aidan was not letting her hand go and it gave her some sense of comfort. Probably if she focused on the feelings his thumb was arousing in her by caressing the side of her palm, she would overcome her panic.

It was working in some way; it was soothing her. But it was as if her subconscious was screaming that something terribly wrong was going to happen and every part of her body was in a defense mode.

"It's okay," the doctor soothed. "I'm going to check your eyes and nothing else, okay?"

She nodded swallowing hard and watched as the doctor pulled down at the skin at the bottom of her eyes and flashed a light to examine them. When he was done, he started something which looked like a recorder and smiled at her.

"Now I want you to focus. Think of something that makes you feel relaxed. Do you remember anything that will make you feel light and dreamy?"

She shook her head. She could not remember anything about her. Was the doctor dumb? But Dr. Landon gently pressed his fingers on her eyelids and massaged her eyelids gently. It gave her a sense of comfort and with her closed eyes, she pictured the shore and waves crashing around. It was relaxing and as she listened to the soft voice speaking to her, she never knew when she started zapping out in another zone.

It was almost like she was floating in the air, her whole body was limp and she could not move an inch.

"What's your name?" she heard someone ask her and she smiled drowsily. That was easy.

"Kate," she replied immediately.

"Your full name."

That too was easy. "Katherine Iris Thornton."

"Where are you from?"

"Manhattan."

There were a few more mundane questions to which she replied almost immediately; Things that she had never realized she already knew about herself. Like what was her first school. Or what was her favourite food. It was not making sense. Even Aidan had never told her about those facts.

"Now Kate. I want you to go back on your wedding day. When you were standing in front of that full length mirror."

She smiled. She could picture herself wearing her tiara of flowers and giggling at her reflection as she waited for Caitlin to get more pins to fix her dress. She never knew she could be so happy. Everything was perfect. Her dress. Her ceremony. Her groom.

"Are you there?" asked the soothing voice.

"Yessss."

"What can you see?"

As she held her bouquet in her hand, she took a step back to admire herself for the hundredth time when she heard a noise behind her. She turned round and saw a well-built man entering the room with a frown.

"There's someone. I don't know his name."

"It does not matter. Can you describe him?"

"He's tall. Quite handsome. And wearing a grey suit."

"Okay. What's he doing?"

"He's asking me why I was not ready yet because my father was waiting for me downstairs. He did not look angry. Just impatient."

"Okay and what did you reply to him?"

Frowning, she tried to focus. She was telling him that they should wait for Caitlin since she had gone to bring a few pins to fix the bottom of her dress. Oh Edward, it would take only three minutes. Pretty please, today's my day.

"Edward. That's what I called him," she announced as soon as she got the information.

"Okay and then?"

Somebody was pounding. It was like a drum beating and she jerked with pain as she realized it was in her head. It was her famous headache returning and she was feeling uneasy again.

"Kate, we need you to focus. Calm down. What can you see now?"

"Edward agreed to wait for Caitlin. We stood for a while waiting for her and I apologized to him. Why did I apologize to him?"

"What did he say?"

"He said it was okay. He was glad for me now since I look so happy. We hugged."

She jerked again not realizing that she was seated.

"What is it? What can you see?" asked the voice immediately placing a light weight in her eyelids again. She fell back on her seat again and tried to calm her erratic breathing and jumping heart. Hell, what was wrong? Then she saw it.

Blood. There was blood everywhere. Edward had been stabbed in the ribs and he fell to the ground bending his body in pain. She stared down at him in horror unable to help him feeling so depressed that she could not even cry. A murder? There had been a murder on her wedding day? And she stood looking down at a dead body wearing her white bridal dress!!!

Then she focused on another detail. Her hands were covered with blood; Edward's blood. If she had not reached out to him when he was wounded, how was her hand covered with blood? The vision was clear; she had stabbed him.

"Kate? Kate?" she heard the voice call out to her. "Do you see someone else in the room?"

There was no one else. It was her the murderer. She had killed someone. She felt her mind black out and suddenly the voice was here again calming her down.

"Kate I want you to come back. Come back to the present. You are visiting me Dr. Landon. Come back now!"

Her throat constricted and she felt her choke as she came back to the present feeling her body wet with perspiration. As she struggled to get back her breath, she focused on the two figures looming over her wearing worried expressions.

"There was no one else," she whispered like a person possessed. "There was no one else. There was no one else. I killed him," she stated in a dead ominous voice.

Oh my God!!! What had she done? She had killed someone?!! That was what she had been running from? Shock grasped her and she could not focus on her surroundings. Who the hell was Edward and why had she killed him?

CHAPTER ELEVEN: KEEP ME SAFE

"Kate!!!" Aidan shouted shaking her but her limp body refused to sustain its position and she fell easily in his arms. Damn! Damn! Damn! They should have ended the session earlier. But they had stalled the hypnosis since she had been so close to the truth.

Whatever she had seen, Aidan could not believe for one second that she was the killer. It was just that she had blocked the trauma about how Edward had been killed and was still unwilling to go down there. It must have been pretty terrifying.

Landon examined her and assured him that she was alright and she only needed some rest. They got another appointment for the next Tuesday and Aidan exited with a quick assurance to the doctor that he would call him back.

His top priority for the moment was Kate. She looked haggard and worn out and he cursed himself for having made her go through such a trauma. But he had not expected the hypnosis session to turn out in that way. He wondered whether her subconscious was blaming her persona for the murder and that was why she had pictured herself as the murderer. It was possible.

He would confirm it with Landon afterwards since he would be more apt to give him a professional overview over the whole matter. Landon had been friends with him for a long time and Aidan knew he could count on his discretion. His doctor friend was among the few persons he could trust in this life.

Glancing sideways, he sighed as he caught sight of the slumped figure of Kate in the car seat right beside him. She was not sleeping but staring in front of her like someone still under the effect of hypnosis. It was hard enough for her to lose her memory and now she looked devastated. As if their lives had not been complicated enough.

And to top it all, it was becoming hard for him to control his urging desires for her. He knew she was also attracted to him; the hot looks she had been sending his way told him everything he needed to know. But fatal attraction was nothing like the love she used to have for him. And unfortunately he was an everything or nothing kind of man.

It was selfish for him to want his Kate back but sleeping with her now could only complicate their already so complicated relationship. She was pretty unstable sometimes and he knew that if they slept together, she would regret it later. Or he would find something missing; something which mattered more to him than anything else. Her undying love for him.

And so he was cursed. He could neither reach out for her nor repel her.

As soon as they reached the cottage, he dropped Kate on her bed to allow her some rest. When he made a move to get up to give her some privacy, she clung to him even in her tired state. Sighing, he decided to stay back until she fell asleep and snuggled closer to her. He could understand her reluctance to be alone. She must be pretty scared after what she had seen and Aidan concluded that she had no idea about the murder before her therapy.

As he laid beside her, he caressed her hair and she fell asleep within seconds. It seemed like the session had worn out all her resources and she did not have enough strength to even talk. But he knew she would have questions for him when she recuperated her energy. And he was mentally preparing himself about how to tackle her when she woke up. It was going to be a clash of the titans between the two of them and he had to make sure he was on her side.

So focused was he on her welfare that he had not realized that the whole episode had tired him too. When he yawned and felt his eyes slumber, he felt the toll of the event catch up with him. And within no time he found himself lost in the usual haze of sleep. It seemed like he had barley closed his eyes when he felt a light caress on his right cheek and he jumped.

It was Kate who had woken up and was admiring him but as soon as his eyes snapped open, she snatched back her hand and retreated back in her shell and he regretted spoiling that moment. During their sleep, she had snuggled close to him and was enwrapped in his arms.

"How are you feeling?" he asked when she made to get up and he retained her by applying some pressure on her back where was his right hand.

"I'm fine. Minus the headache," she mumbled her voice husky from sleep and he could find nothing sexier. He had always loved to wake with her, her hair tumbled and eyes drowsy as her eyes looked up at him with love and admiration. Everything was same except for the expression of love which was missing. And he was not liking it one bit.

So he decided to do something about it.

Bending down, he brushed his lips to hers and watched as her eyes rounded in surprise her lips forming a most obvious O. Smiling, he winked at her trying to lighten the atmosphere but preparing himself for the storm that he was sure was yet to come. When she did not make any comment, he shifted down on the bed and pressed her head on his chest.

They stayed intertwined like that before she finally asked the question he had been dreading to hear for a long time.

"What happened back at the house?" she asked in a trembling voice and he tightened his grasp on her elbows to offer her some support. "Was there really a murder?"

She was still lying with her head crooked on his shoulder and he could not see her face. But if her pounding heartbeats were any indication, the question meant a lot to her. And he decided to come clean with her. No need to prevaricate now as she had seen the murder in her hypnosis. It must have felt as real as the first time.

"Yes," he answered simply not knowing what other explanation to give her.

He felt her tense and her heartbeats pick up speed even more of that was possible. He wished he could read her mind so that he could offer her the appropriate words. He would have known what to say exactly with his old Kate. But he was still teetering with this new version of her, it was like he was treading on broken shells.

In any case, it was not a very easy task to watch his love suffer like that.

"Who was Edward?" she asked her voice still muffled.

"Edward Bigfoot was your ex."

At that, she lifted her head to watch him. Probably to make up her mind whether he was lying or not. And her eyes were suspiciously misty. All Aidan wanted to do was to hug her close and offer her every assurance she might need from him.

"My ex-fiancé, right?" she repeated her eyes round in wonder. "The one I ditched at the altar for you?"

"Yah. The very one," he said wincing at her exaggerated version. He had related to her about the cancelled wedding when they had first met at the convent.

She sighed heavily obviously drawing her own conclusions. "We must have been in pretty bad terms. B...but," her voice faltered. "..I cannot believe I killed him."

"You did not!" he protested hotly.

She frowned at him. "I saw it, remember? It was me. There was no one else in that fitting room," she replied getting herself in a frenzied state. It was like he had feared; now that she knew of the murder, it was going to be difficult to control her.

"Kate, you must have been mistaken."

Adamantly, she shook her head. "It was clear. I had blood all over me. It was his blood. Oh my God! I can still smell that damned smell. And why didn't you tell me about the murder before?" she shouted at him but could not release his grip no matter how much she struggled.

Finally exhausted, she gave up and poked him in the rib as a means of retribution.

"I could not," he admitted wearily. "You were already in a state of shock so I decided to wait until I had some more clues about the murder."

She closed her eyes in dismay. "No wonder you were so unwilling to get me back. It was to protect me, right? To keep them from putting me in jail?"

Once again he noted that even with her amnesia, she was smart enough to conclude the truth. It was better for him to come out with the real truth because knowing Kate she would not rest until she found out everything. And besides it might help to jog her memory back.

"The police is suspecting you. And yes this is the reason I decided to stay back. There is no other finger print or blood sample found apart from yours."

Kate sucked in a loud breath absorbing the shocking news he had just delivered. He knew he was aggravating the situation but he had no other choice than spilling the beans now.

"How is the Bigfoot family coping with things? You said we were family friends. D...do they blame me too for their son's murder?" she asked looking so forlorn that he felt her pain.

And he told her the truth. How Abigail Bigfoot is still not in talking terms with the family yet and carefully omitting the fact that they had even filed a case against her. It was not that he was lying to her but there were some information that he still had to keep unrevealed for the sake of her own sanity.

"Is there anything else you're hiding from me? Please tell me. I'm okay now. But I need to know everything because it might help me remember."

"There's nothing else. I have not started to investigate on the murder yet because my main focus is you. All I wanted was to find you and now that I have, all I want is for you to get fine. I have faith, I am sure whoever has done this terrible thing will eventually pay."

"You are not getting the point here Aidan," she said frustrated. "I killed him!"

"Will you stop that?" he muttered crossly.

At his words, she disentangled herself free from his embrace and sat up on the bed which creaked a little. "What do you mean? It's clear to me that I killed him. Maybe he had been hitting on me or something and things got ugly. But whatever happened back then, I should not have killed him. I mean he was after all…"

"Kate, you did not kill him. I'm hundred percent sure of that fact."

"How can you be so sure?" she retorted back. "Even the police found no other suspect and they are looking for me. My future is ruined. And I can't even remember the damned reason why I did it," she fumed and Aidan knew she was terribly affected.

Katherine Thornton was not one used to rant usually.

"I will never believe for one second that you could kill someone. I'm your fiancé, remember? I know you better than anyone. You can never do intentional harm since you have no evil soul in you. I could vouch for that fact with my life," he professed getting over emotional at the intensity of his words.

She seemed taken aback and gazed at him in amazement. "What about all the proofs that are hinting otherwise? You cannot disregard them."

He scoffed. "What proofs? The police have not even bothered to start an enquiry or making sure that there was another person involved;

they're too busy looking for you. And considering how fast I found you, they are doing a pathetic job out of it. But they won't even consider any other option that is why they are stressing on you," he finished feeling even more frustrated that she could believe she would kill someone.

"What about my vision?"

"What about it?" he repeated his frustration building up another notch.

"How was I covered with blood if I had not touched him after he fell down?" she asked. "Earlier in my nightmares I used to wonder why I was stabbed but could not feel the pain. It was because the one stabbed was Edward and not me. Except my mind could not remember that fact at that time!" she exclaimed frustration laced in her voice too reflecting his exact feelings.

"But maybe your mind is blocking that part. Because during the session you said you were hugging after you apologized to him."

She frowned as if picturing her vision once again. "Yah," she finally said morosely not liking the reminder of the whole event.

"And suddenly Edward is stabbed with a kitchen knife. Where the hell did you get a knife when you were going to be married in a few minutes? How could you suddenly stab a knife at him? There must be a part of the puzzle missing here. And it's the crucial part."

"You are playing the devil's advocate here just to protect me. Please let us go back and I will surrender to the police," she suddenly said and Aidan could have strangled her.

"Are you out of your mind? Do you know what you're asking of me? Letting you spend some time in jail will just kill me. Not to forget the fact that the killer will still get back to you when he knows you're still alive."

"But..."

"Nothing doing. If the police catches up with us, you can use your memory loss as an excuse. Don't; worry I promise everything will work out fine. Just give me some time to trace the murderer. Ryce has been on certain trails but they have all died up after some time. Whoever has pulled up such a stunt must have been pretty clever."

"Or you might be completely mistaken. What if Edward had tried something with me and I stabbed him in defense?"

Aidan frowned at her obstinacy on believing she was the killer but to certain extent he could understand her. She was someone without memory and the first thing she remembered was a murder and her as only participant. For one, she no longer knew herself and second she was still too under the shock to think correctly.

"What about the sadistic laughter that you seemed to hear in the background every time?" he countered suddenly remembering the only fact that would play in his favor.

And he was right. That argument seemed to sober her up and he watched fascinated as her forehead creased in concentration and finally she gave up. Even in such a serious and dramatic moment, he was founding her cute.

"I guess you're right," she finally conceded not sounding completely convinced.

"I know I'm right. There no bloody way you could have killed someone," he replied and made to get up as his growling tummy informed him it was noon. He should prepare some food soon as his hunger would end up killing him. Or maybe they could order for lunch today. He was still too tired to think rationally.

"Isn't that love talking?" she asked and he froze at the words.

Love... So she realized that he loved her now. It was a big leap forward and he never wanted to let that moment go. Slowly almost afraid that if he hastened, something might break the atmosphere, he turned to face her. She was wearing a slight tentative smile.

"It could be," he said ruefully afraid to take his next breath waiting in anticipation of what her next words would be. "But I believe in you more than anything." And then she did something completely out of the norm.

In one abrupt movement, she jumped on him making him lose his balance and fall down on the bed with him pinned under her. Tying her hand behind his neck, she brought his face closer and kissed him soundly on the lips. Like a smack.

He grinned and hugged her back but then their chemistry went out of control as usual. The spark she had set blew out of proportion and he felt himself harden to the point of his lower part paining. He willed himself to control his violent urge to pounce on her once more and looked up at her with fire in his eyes.

"Kate…"

"I know," she whispered back and he lost all his senses.

Grabbing her, he plunged his tongue into her mouth and received the same special treatment. She smelled of peaches as always and he was drugged with her essence. The emotion was familiar but no less intense. He felt himself lost in the whirlwind of sensations going crazy with need.

But taking a deep breath, he stepped back taking short breaths trying to calm his raging senses. He could not repeat the mistake of last time. He had to know.

"Kate, are you sure?" he asked.

She nodded and he kissed her again seeping the very essence from her. He was like a starved man having been deprived of food for far too long. Letting go of every rational thoughts, he slowed down his kisses taking his time to explore her delectable mouth. Even if she was behaving like she was not used to responding to kisses, it was arousing the hell out of him.

When finally, after several mind-blowing kisses he could wait no longer, he put his hand under her top to caress her flat tummy. The feel of her naked skin nearly made him feel like a werewolf finally taking its full form. And she must have felt the heat because she hissed and the effect of the sound made him nearly have an orgasm. It was so hot and sultry.

When his hands reached her bra, he took his time to tease her and when she moaned for more, he removed the top in one movement and bent to bite her lightly on her bra. She groaned out loud and grabbed his head closer.

It was all encouragement he needed. With one deft movement, he unclasped the undergarment and devoured the two creamy feasts in front of him. Pleasuring her had always given him more pleasure and her moans were making him even more horny.

When the peaks became so rigid that it perked around her mold, he sucked on them with a devotion he had never attributed them before. They tasted just like her. Sweet and unique. For how long he lavished on them, he had no idea but he knew she was aroused to the point of no return when she whimpered beneath him like someone possessed.

Taking the cue, he unfastened her jeans but faltered when she placed a hand on his. Still lost in the haze of desire, he looked up at her uncomprehendingly and saw the expression on her face. It was like she was afraid.

Letting out a harsh expletive, he wrenched himself from her before he did something he would regret. Sitting on the edge of the bed, he placed his head in his hand trying to calm his raging breathing. She wanted to stop now? When he was ready to explode with desire. What the hell was she playing at?

CHAPTER TWELVE: TO LOVE AGAIN

Kate could have killed herself as she stared at the desolate figure sitting on the edge of the bed in acute pain. It made her feel a deep pinch in her heart and guilt replaced the initial mortification. What the hell was wrong with her? She knew she should not have started anything she could not finish and it only made her a tease.

But he had been so irresistible. Irresistible in the sense that she felt wonderful at the kind of trust he had in her. And wished she could trust him back like that. Suddenly, Kate started to wish fervently that she got her memory back because she knew she was missing something important here. It made her realize how much he loved her and she could not play with his feelings because she was not sure if she loved him that much.

Looking at the forlorn figure in front of her, Kate wished she could undo the past. How stupid could she be? Why the hell had she been unable to resist him like that? Hell, she loved the way they interacted and guessed that they must have a pretty good understanding under normal circumstances.

Normal circumstances being if she had not lost her memory. It was starting to become the problem of her life and she could not imagine how to handle it anymore. What if she never got her memory back? Would he still love her anyway?

She knew that whenever they were together although it was very subtle he was expecting his Kate back. And it hurt her to know that she was not enough for him now. The Kate she was now was just a shadow of the Kate she had been. It was silly fighting with herself but she was jealous of the other Kate. Who had never been a part of her since her memory loss.

Why the hell did Aidan love her so much? Why couldn't he love her now? As she was? Then she suddenly she realized the stark truth about herself. Why she was feeling so low and so helpless. Why she was jealous of her own self? It was simply because she had fallen in love with him.

That had to be it. She had fallen head over heels in love with him. As if it had not been enough she had lost her memory, she had lost her heart too on the way. And he loved her back except she was no longer herself. Hell, what a mess!

As she absorbed the shock, she tried to school her features into a impossible mask not wanting him to know that she had been foolish enough to fall in love with him. She had to had a prep talk to herself first before she could say anything to him. She wanted some time alone to reorder her thoughts and confirm her feelings for him.

Finally, he lifted his head and looked at her with his jaws clenched. Kate felt like her heart was hanging in open air as he looked at her in his intense way and after a long time he finally said.

"Try to get some rest. I'm going to prepare us some lunch."

She knew she should be relieved that he had not brought up what just transpired between them. But instead when he did not bother mentioning it, she felt like it was all insignificant to him. Damn, she was so confused.

"Would the old Kate let you prepare lunch?" she asked feeling piqued that he had not commented on her restraint - or lack of.

He seemed caught unaware at the answer and shook his head. "Kate was..." and stopped as he realized his mistake. He was even starting to speak of her in the third person now. "I mean you are a good cook and would never have let me set foot in the kitchen."

It was said matter-of-factly; neither with remorse nor reproach. Yet, she felt the words pierce her heart as the meaning of the words seep in. It meant that he was not even expecting things from her as he would have from his old Kate. And she was starting to get tired of thinking of Kate like she was someone else. Hell, she was Kate!!!

"Alright, then," she said leaping off the bed and stopped at the door looking behind to find a stunned looking Aidan. "I'm preparing lunch," she stated and without giving him time to reply, she fled to the kitchen not wanting him to catch up any of her inner turmoil.

Finally she had a few moment alone to herself. Breathing hard, she tried to calm her heartbeats and swallowed past her parched throat. It had to be love; the way her eyes always looked for him. Her heart beats rocketed every time he was near. Or her hand moistened each time those green eyes focused on her.

Thankfully, she still remembered how to cook and started to smash some potatoes to make a gravy. There was bread on the marble and she decided to make something light as it was already late. She must be used to cooking because she was doing things automatically while her mind was still on her problem at hand.

How could she confess her feelings to him when she was still unsure whether she was a killer or not? Unlike him, she had not absolved herself from the possibility that she might be the murderer of Edward and she knew that sooner or later she would have to face the consequences.

What if they never found someone else as culprit? The police would be sure to apprehend her as they could not remain in hiding forever. What would happen then?

It was not fair to him to get his love back to lose it all over again. She would have to better control her emotions and not let him know that she had feelings for him. She turned at the sound of someone approaching and smiled absent-mindedly at him trying to keep a casual composure.

"Lunch nearly ready," she babbled not meeting his eyes. "I haven't prepared anything special since it's already two and..."

She stopped as he stopped close behind her while she stood facing the sink with her back to him. She was trapped and if she moved she would have to move closer to him. And it would be the death of her. At his closeness, her heart had literally stopped beating and she could no longer feel her legs. All she wanted to do was to lean back on him and feel him. It was lethal.

Her hazy eyes snapped open at his next words. "What happened back then?" he asked in a voice oh-so light that she had to brace herself at the impact of his words.

Resisting the urge to whirl round and face him, she placed both her hands on the side of the sink and leaned forward to prevent herself from swaying towards him. She had to clear that fog of desire which overwhelmed her every time he approached her. It was almost like a hypnosis.

What was the question again?

"I know you felt something too," he went on when she did not reply. "Then suddenly something went wrong. Care to explain?"

She gulped. Explain what? That she had the hots for him? That she loved him but did not know if she was a killer? That she could not be selfish enough to drag him in the dilemma she found herself in? That she was a cursed person with no past and no future.

She had only the present and she was with him. And that was where she would like to stay forever. He made her feel beautiful and it was the most sensational feeling in the world. And she wanted to feel like that forever. Except that it was not possible; not while she was unsure of her innocence.

"I'm sorry," she said finally. "I shouldn't have led you on like that."

"That's not the answer to my question. Why did you stop? I thought you were enjoying it," he taunted his voice becoming laced with sexual tension again.

"I wasn't" she lied promptly.

"No?" he asked in a challenging way and she had a flash of him looking down at her with his eyebrows cocked even without turning round.

And felt his hand lightly caress her back. It sent goose bumps all down to her spine and she had to make a Herculean effort not to shiver at his touch. He moved closer; so close that she could feel the heat emanating from his body.

"Why did you stop?" he repeated the words so close to her ears that she could not help the shiver than rippled through her body this time. Damn! Just when she had thought she had escaped that question.

"I don't know," she replied closing her eyes in dismay. "I.. I can never be your Kate," she finally confessed in a small voice. "No matter how hard I'm trying, I know there's something you're expecting from me…"

The sentence hung unfinished in the air and she forgot to breathe as she waited for his answer. Praying. Hoping. That she was wrong.

She felt his hand on her shoulder and he gently turned her round and she watched the expression in his eyes. They glittered as they looked at her with tenderness and love and she felt her eyes weld with his like they were one. His every feelings were communicated to her in that one deep look and she felt like she was being reassured even if there was not one single word has been uttered from his mouth.

"Kate…" he simply said and closed her eyes waiting for the inevitable kiss.

When their lips touched again, she felt his now familiar taste which was becoming fast addictive. When the butterfly kisses were not enough, she opened her mouth for more and as his tongue dipped into her mouth, she felt his love pour out from him and his every feeling being conveyed in that one kiss.

It tasted better than anything else and even without her memory she knew there was nothing in the whole world which could match the sensations that were rippling through her at that precise moment.

Finally, he broke the kiss and looked down at her his eyes still shining with the same emotions. "I love you Kate. How can you doubt that?"

"Do you?" she asked uncertainly. "What if I never got my memory back? Will you still love me? Will you be able to accept me as I am?"

It was a question she had to ask. She had to know if he would love her even if she did not remember him; even if she was unable to remember her past eventually.

He sighed in guise of answer and she felt her heart sink. Would he disappoint her? If he said something about how she had changed and he still loved her, she would not digest it. It would not be credible; she could not believe that someone could love her when she was a totally different person.

"Kate," he repeated more firmly this time. "You silly woman. You haven't changed that much. You look the same, you taste the same. Hell, you feel the same. You're still the same Kate except with no memories of us. And it does not matter."

Well she had felt different; she never knew she was still the same Kate to him. It felt wonderful to know that even with her memory loss, he still considered her to be the same person she was. Finally, she was able to understand the kind of love he harbored for her. It was simply epic.

"You mean that?" she asked in wonder.

"Of course," he growled. "You're no different to me and I'm a better judge than that. You don't remember yourself, right?" he asked ruefully.

"Right," she repeated still dazed. She could not believe that he loved her so much; it simply felt so wonderful to at the receptive end of so much love. And for the first time since the whole nightmare had begun, Kate felt happiness surround her heart. She wanted to trust him to believe every of his word. If he said she was not the murderer, then she wanted to believe him.

And to think she had once doubted him. Had believed that he was the murderer; the one who was trying to harm her. It seemed ludicrous now as he was the one to help her heal her emotional wounds. It did not matter if she remembered or not. It did not even matter if she had killed someone. He still loved her anyway.

A bout of happiness engulfed her and she hugged him tightly. "I love you too," she said smiling against his shoulder.

She heard his scoff and she stepped back from his embrace feeling stunned and a bit silly. She had just confessed her love for him and he was ridiculing her?

"What?" she asked looking at him in a self-conscious way.

"Nothing," he replied in a self-deprecatory tone which matched the scoff. "I thought I heard you say that you loved me too."

"I did," she told him. "I mean I do. I did say that I love you because I do love you."

"Seriously?!!" he shrieked in a loud tone. "When? How?"

She had to laugh at the cutest expression on his face. He was flabbergasted by her announcement and she felt so happy that she feared her heart might explode anytime.

"I felt attracted to you since day one," she confessed shyly falling back in his arms.

"You mean when I gagged you to prevent you from shouting?" he mocked.

She giggled. It did sounded more like a thriller than a love story. "No, silly. When you came to visit Mother Katherine the first time. I was watching you from the corridor."

"I knew there was someone watching me. I felt like somebody was lurking behind that wall. If only I knew it was you…"

"I'm sorry," she said sobering up. "I thought you were the one trying to kill me at that time," she replied. "I was not thinking straight; I was only running from someone dangerous. And from what I had seen in my nightmares, I was crying out your name just before the knife pierced through my ribs."

Aidan frowned at her and she knew she was not making sense. So she explained to him how at first she had thought that she was crying out the murderer's name and Mother Katherine had told her she might be calling someone for help.

"So this confirms that you had nothing to do with the murder," Aidan informed her and she stopped talking not quite following his logic. The question must have been obvious on her face because he replied before she had time to formulate it.

"You did say that you were running from someone dangerous, right? So it's clear that you felt that your life was in danger too. If you have killed Edward, you would be running from yourself and even if you were traumatized by the event, you wouldn't have this irrational fear that someone if after you."

Kate sighed. It made sense. But Aidan would find any detail enough to absolve her anyway. And she did not want to think about that for the time being. She had…other more important issue to attend. Like the hard bulge protruding near her thighs and making her almost dizzy with desire.

"Let's go upstairs," she whispered planting a quick kiss on his cheek and he looked at her in surprise and mockery.

"Are you sure?"

She laughed. "Let's eat first. I'm hungry," she prevaricated shyly not raising to his bait.

Food tasted like cotton because all she had on mind was the delicious looking man in front of her. She would not mind having him for lunch instead. She could not believe how horny she felt at the thought of what would happen in a few moments. It was as if she was another appetite was becoming more poignant.

"Let's go," he finally said his voice full of sexual tension. And when he picked her up in his arms, she clung to him like he was a lifeline.

When he laid her down on the bed, she settled back to find a comfortable position and felt lonely when he did not join her immediately. Peeping, she tried to figure out what he was doing but he had his back to her and she could not see anything. It looked like he was removing something from the drawer or something.

"Before I forget..." he said his back still to her. "Here are your things."

She sat up to better see what he had brought for her and squealed in excitement as he produced a ring. It looked like an engagement ring with a diamond on the center and diamond dust on the side. It must be her engagement ring; the one she had never found on her left finger and had assumed that she had flung on her fiancé's face.

"How come it's with you? I thought I lost it," she said smiling as he slipped it back on her left finger and she felt a sense of good feeling as the ring fell back in its place.

"You gave it to me to find a matching wedding ring. I was supposed to give it back to you but I forgot since I chose the wedding ring at the last moment."

Happy, she watched the light being reflected in the gem and it was the exact replica of what she was feeling. Shining and beautiful.

"Oh thank you Aidan."

He kissed her playfully on her nose. "It's baby. You always call me baby."

Her smile grew wider. "Really? And what do you call me?"

"Katie. My little Katie."

"What's in your hand again?" she asked suddenly seeing his hand sneak to snatch something from the drawer near her.

Without replying, he showed her the object which was in his hand and she could have cried when she remembered what it was. .It was the small chain she had sold to the jeweler for her survival. He had got it back for her.

"Where did you get that?"

"I found it at the jewelry store where you left it. That is where I found your trail. I gifted it to you for your birthday when we were at the university," he said turning her round and making her wear it.

"No wonder. I knew it was special to me," she replied admiring it on her neck and suddenly all thoughts of jewelry fled from her mind as she felt his lips on her nape.

"Don't ever leave it behind. It was the symbol of my love for you even before I realized that I loved you," he said his voice sounding emotional.

"I love you," she told him caressing his cheeks glad that she could say the words freely.

"Oh Katie. Welcome back," Aidan said kissing her fervently and the rest of their problems faded as they got lost in each other. It was as if they were one; it was difficult for her to say where she started and where he ended.

CHAPTER THIRTEEN: GOT YOU BACK

There was an obvious change about her. Not in her personality but in the way she behaved. It was as if her love for him had set her free and she was no longer hesitant to explore her past. Or her sexuality. And she was more feisty than the Kate he had known.

And he was starting to like it too damn much. So much that he almost forgot the problems impending on them like a heavy rain ready to drench them anytime. He wanted them to stay in that cottage forever. To stay like that forever.

When she had confessed her love to him, it had been so unexpected that he had thought it was his imagination at first. Never in his wildest dreams had he thought that Kate would end up falling with him all over again even with her memory gone. It humbled him to be loved so much by someone so wonderful as her.

And could not contain his immense joy when she had confirmed her love for him; it meant that whatever happened between them, they were always meant to be together. He had missed her so much that now he had found her, he never wanted to lose her again.

Consequently, so happy had he been in his love cocoon that he had completely forgotten about his next appointment with Dr. Landon. Thankfully, he had put a reminder and when his phone buzzed to tell him that it was time for the appointment, he felt all the pressure coming back. It was time for another painful session and it would tear him to see Kate in anguish yet again.

But he knew he had to be strong for her; he had to be rock solid to enable her to lean on him in her weakest moment. No matter how they tried to avoid the real problem, they had to tackle it eventually and his next step was to bring her for another session to Landon.

Aidan did not want her glow of happiness to dim when he told her about the impending appointment. But surprisingly, she took it well and calmly in complete contrast as to what he was expecting.

"Are you nervous?" he asked when she joined him in the car.

She let out a dry laugh. "I am. But I want to get on with it. I know it's the only thing to do for the time being since Ryce is still stuck up with the list you made him," she replied.

She was referring to his list of enemies he had prepared when he had believed that Kate was kidnapped. At that time, Aidan had wanted to go in that direction to look for Kate when Ryce had managed to convince him that he had been carrying it too far. But eventually defeated with the local police's attitude, Ryce had himself started to follow that trail and Aidan had been forced to tell him that he had found Kate back.

To say that Ryce had been furious would be the understatement of the year.

"Whattt??!!! Are you f**cking kidding me here? I have…"

"I know. Listen, I should apologize but I was not going to take any risk. I mean she had forgotten everything. How was I supposed to react? I wanted to protect and get her well."

"But Wolf you could have told me. I thought I was your ally. I mean you could have at least told someone. Do you know how everyone is worried about Kate? And you. You have disappeared with no news whatsoever."

"I know. I know. But I had no choice. If we came back, you would want me to go after the killer and I did not want that. Kate is my priority."

Ryce sighed. It was a positive sign when Ryce sighed. It meant that he was giving in except he was making sure the person receiving the sigh knew he was not totally agreeing.

"How the hell did you find her? And when?"

"I found her on the day I disappeared," he replied closing his eyes in dismay. He could feel another outraged cry on its way. And right it was!

"Two weeks?!! You have found her since two weeks?! And here I thought you were following your stupid trail of business enemies."

"I'm sorry. I couldn't tell you about Kate," he replied not knowing what else to say. He knew he had messed up but given another chance he would have still repeated the same mistake. He still believed that Kate was the one who should be kept safe and to hell with everyone else.

"I understand man. But I was worried sick about Kate. Even Jennifer never stops calling every day to ask me if I have found anything about her friend."

Aidan felt bad for having hidden that from him. It wasn't that he was not trusting him but it would have been a risk. Like it was now. The more person knew about Kate, the more dangerous it was for them to stay at the cottage. And that was why he had omitted mentioning where he was staying. Not to Ryce and not to Alex Thornton.

"Yes I know everyone's worried. But Ryce there had been a murder at the castle. I cannot risk Kate's life again; at least not when she's suffering from amnesia. She's defenseless and if I had brought her back to the castle, she would not have known whom to beware of."

"She does not remember anything?"

"No, not even us. And just imagine how hard it would have been for her to doubt her own family who are only strangers to her now."

Again he heard his friend's loud sigh. Aidan knew he was not far from convincing him completely that he had done the right thing.

"And besides, the minute we returned back to the castle or penthouse, the local police would have apprehended Kate. You know that they are not willing to do anything else other than suspecting Kate as the prime culprit."

"Yeah. I'm glad to know she's safe. And Jen would be…"

"You cannot tell her!" Aidan protested as soon as he guessed that the next second, his friend was going to call his wife to inform him that Kate was with amnesia. Like it was some fancy party! Had he been talking to a wall during the whole time here?

"Man, can you understand that someone is trying to kill her? And I don't want anyone else to know that she's been found," he practically shouted feeling angry that Ryce could not understand that much. Was it too much to ask from his friend to keep his mouth shut. He knew everybody was worried about Kate but if he had not informed Judith about Kate, he thought everyone else could bloody wait.

They had enough problems already and he wished Ryce would stop behaving like a husband and more like a friend to Kate. He knew it was going to be difficult for Jennifer to be far from everyone but eventually Aidan was saving her life too. What if the killer decided to get to her family to track Kate down?

"What do you mean? Are you having doubts on us as well? Is that it? You don't want me or Jen to know because you think we could be the one..."

"Don't be silly," he retorted back. Why the hell was Ryce complicating things further. Of course Ryce and Jen had nothing to do with the murder. "But I know that whoever has killed Bigfoot is smart enough to cover his tracks. And he will strike again as soon as we make the tiniest mistake. What if he tries to harm Jen? Or Flint?!"

Ryce remained silent and Aidan knew he had gotten to him this time. Finally, Ryce accepted his explanation asking how he could help them.

"Stay close to the local police. And gather maximum information you can. I phone Alex regularly and he keeps me updated. I would want you to go after the first suspect of the list I had drafted you. Because since we have nothing to do, we'd better start with something."

Ryce agreed gruffly but Aidan knew he was still pissed with him for having hidden the truth. Hell, had he been in the reverse position, Aidan was sure he would have felt the same way too. Well, it would take some time for Ryce to ultimately realize that it had been his only choice. But he was still sorry to put his friend in such a delicate situation.

"Ryce..." he said after they had everything planned out. "I'm really sorry about hiding the truth from you. But I had no other choice. I am not willing to take any risk; not with Kate's life. I was going to phone you but then I thought of Flint and decided it would be better if you ignored the truth. I would request you to please not say anything to Jen."

"Yah ok I understand. Please keep her safe. For everyone's sake." And those were the last words they spoke.

So far, he had no news of Ryce again and he had concluded that the trail had not been a successful one; his business rivals were not vile enough to kill. Although he had known it was already a lost case, he had insisted on Ryce going with the enquiry because they had no other option for the time being.

His thoughts were interrupted when he realized that they were in front of the doctor's office. He had been so lost in the past that had not spoken a word during the whole trip. Filled with remorse, he threw a furtive glance in her direction but she seemed to be lost in her thoughts too. As guise of repentance, he held her hand to show her his undying support.

She sent a reassuring look in his direction and squeezed back his hand. Words were futile since he could not offer her the comfort she needed. She had to face her past else they would never be able to move on.

As soon as they reached the doctor's waiting room though, Kate started to fidget and Aidan got worried about her. He knew it was going to be the hardest thing she might come to face in her life and he was going to be there for her.

"Do you want to go through this? I swear if you don't want this we will go back and think of something else."

But before he had even finished his sentence, Kate was shaking her head vehemently. "It's alright. I've reached a point where I want to remember now. I want to remember us and everything else. Don't worry, it will turn out fine."

Aidan could not help smiling; instead of him comforting her this time it was the reverse. He was glad that Kate was feeling stronger now because he felt that his resolve was draining away little by little. It had not been easy for him to bear all of the tragic events alone.

"Don't worry," she repeated seeming to pick his fatigue. "I promise I'll be fine."

"Sure, let's wait for the doctor to call us then," he led the way to the waiting room where they sat on a couch facing each other with apprehension filled eyes. No one dared say anything because each one knew that words would not be able to appease what they would go through in the next moment.

When Landon called them for another session, he felt his heart heavy with worry and watched helpless as Kate once again sat on the armchair. Within seconds, Kate got back her dazed expression like the first time and Aidan knew the exact moment she zapped out.

Landon was asking her mundane questions just like last time and she was replying back. It was amazing how she knew everything about herself in her sleep. Things he had never told her after her amnesia. It meant that she remembered everything except that it was stuck somewhere in her subconscious.

Finally, they came to the session in the fitting room where Edward had joined her while she had been waiting for Caitlin. That time

Landon skipped the time when she was standing in front of the mirror and came directly to the point where she was hugging Edward. When she related the scenario again, nothing had changed except that she added a few details here and there which did not serve any help whatsoever.

"I am hugging him and I am feeling sorry that I have let him down," she was saying her voice seemed almost husky with sleep. It was the repetition of what had happened last time. Aidan braced himself for what was going to happen this time. But could not help feeling disappointment fill him with her next words.

Just like last time, she became agitated but saw the same thing she had. "There's blood everywhere."

Landon looked over at him with a look that spoke volume. It was like last time. She had skipped the exact moment when the murder had taken place. She was still blocking that part of her memory and it was difficult for her to release the repressed event.

It was a bad sign. If she remained stuck up like that, they would never be able to move on without hurting herself. The last time they had spoken, Landon had warned him that it would not be easy for her if she was still blocking on the murder the second time. He would have to probe and it would be even more difficult for her.

And that was why Landon was giving him the look. The doctor was asking him whether he could go ahead with asking her some more questions to unblock that part of her memory. Unable to take a decision, he looked down at the white face of his beloved on the armchair as she was jerking off the memory.

And finally swallowing hard, he nodded to allow him to proceed with the questions. It was going to be hard but it was something that had to be done.

"Kate, why is there so much blood?" Landon asked and Kate stopped her abrupt movements and frowned lightly as if trying to figure out the answer.

"I... I don't know. I...I..."

"Okay, relax. Who is with you in the room apart from Edward? Is there someone else?"

The sentence hung in the air for such a long time that Aidan feared she might not respond to the question. It was the question which would confirm that whether she had been the murderer or not. Even if he was sure she was not the killer, he wanted her to at least see someone else in the picture. It would be a start even if she had a mere flash.

Then she replied in a low voice almost as if she herself had just found the answer. "Yes. Yes there is someone else."

"Who is it, Kate?"

"I can't see him. He...he...," she stammered and Aidan watched as the doctor pressed a light finger on her head. At least they knew the killer was a male.

"Concentrate Kate. You were hugging Edward in the fitting room. What happened then?"

She jerked again more violently this time and Aidan knew it was time. She was seeing what she had been blocking all the time.

"Someone came from behind. I can see someone behind Edward's back." She paused. 'There is something wrong with this picture."

"What's wrong Kate? What happened?"

"He's got a knife," she said sounding somewhat angry. "He's right behind you, Edward. There's a knife. Beware!" she shouted and Aidan guessed that those were the words she had uttered at that time.

"No! No!" she cried. "He has stabbed him. The bloody bastard! I am afraid. He has stabbed Edward in the ribs from behind. How is this possible? Oh my God!" she cried tears streaming down her cheeks.

"Kate…Kate…" Landon was crying but she was not responding. It was as if she was still traumatized by everything and she had suddenly relived that instant.

"Stop it now Landon," Aidan said intervening for the first time during the whole session. He could see that Kate was getting more agitated and could guess what had happened next. The killer must have made a dive for her and she was now trying to defend herself. He did not want her to live that traumatic event over and over again.

"He's after me!" she suddenly cried. "He wants to kill me," she repeated. "It's a kitchen knife," she jerked again on the armchair and hurt her head. But she was in such a trance that she did not realize that her head had knocked against the chair. Aidan could have it no more.

"Stop it now, Landon," he barked in a voice that brooked no argument rushing to steady her. Without wasting time, the doctor started to soothe Kate by asking her to come back. Kate resisted as she was still in her hypnotic state and was not listening to them.

Aidan called himself all kinds of fools for he had been the one who had allowed Kate to continue with the session. Hell, he should have been more careful and stopped her when there was still time. What if she got even more affected after the last session?

After several minutes, she finally calmed down and was relaxed again. Aidan feel his heart coming back to a normal pace as relief seep in. Kate was okay. It was all that mattered. They would continue the session some other time. Or they might never need to do another session again.

The surprising thing was that never once had Kate mentioned who was the killer. She would have told them if she knew something about the attacker. It was weird and maybe when she woke up he would ask her more about the criminal. They had something to work on anyway and with that new evidence, he might even consider take Kate back home to the local police.

As he watched, Kate she came back to the present when the doctor asked her and her eyes opened in a jerk as if she was waking up from a nightmare.

"Aidan!" she cried as soon as she opened her eyes to him. And looked at him with something akin to panic in her golden eyes. Kneeling beside her, he caressed her hair lightly and smiled reassuringly at her.

"I'm right here baby. It's okay. I'm here. I won't let anything happen to you,' he soothed and dried off her tears that were streaming down her cheeks. It did not matter if she was not seeing the killer. It did not matter if she could not get further from that.

He would fight the whole world for her. Now that she knew she was not the murderer, he was sure he could take the recent discovery to the police. Whatever was waiting for them in the future, he was sure he would never let her down.

But enough was enough. He would never let her sit for another session again. That last session had usurped all her energy and she sat sagged against the armchair sweat dripping down her face. It had exhausted her,

"Aidan," she repeated squeezing his hand hard in an attempt to get his undivided attention and he looked at her expecting her to say something.

And said the words he had been longing to hear for a long time now.

"Aidan, I remember everything."

CHAPTER FOURTEEN: MOOT POINT

After having blurted out the first thing that came in her mind, Kate watched as extreme happiness filled Aidan's face. Her Aidan. Her beloved. How the hell could she have forgotten him? Everything was clearer now. Her past, her life, her spoilt wedding.

"Are you okay?' he asked her still holding her hand and she nodded getting down the armchair. Feeling a bout of dizziness, she had to steady herself for a few seconds before putting on a brave smile. Even with her memory back, she was still feeling that fatigue and ever present headache.

Groggily, she nodded and leant against Aidan for support. She was feeling so tired and mentally drawn. "I'm fine," she replied unwilling to look at anything or anyone other than Aidan. It seemed like it had been ages since she had last seen him and some part of her had missed him.

Certain things were still indistinct in her mind and she was still unable to bridge the gap between some events. For instance, it was difficult to discern what had happened just after she had run from the murderer. All she remembered was that she had been so scared and thanking God that she had managed to escape.

"Aidan, I...I... don't remember what happened after I ran from the wedding. I'm so sorry darling to have left you like that."

"That's ok. I know you had no choice. You were trying to save your life," he replied back and then turned to the doctor to ask for some hints about her health.

The doctor was explaining that those were normal symptoms and she was not really paying attention. She was mortified to realize what Aidan must have endured. It was hard to imagine what he must have felt when he had known that his bride was missing. And that too on his own wedding day.

It must have been such an ordeal for him. But like he said she had no choice. It had been the only thing she could have thought of to save her life. Even now when she was trying to think about what happened, the headache was back with a vengeance and she asked the doctor if it was normal that she had this chronic headache again.

She was informed that she had to rest to gain back some energy and must not stress herself. After prescribing some medicines, Dr. Landon asked them to visit him again and Aidan took her back to the car while he fetched the pills to cure her headache.

It was all she wanted for the time being. And true to her needs, as soon as she swallowed some of the pills back home, her eyes and mind shut down to oblivion. She never knew when she fell asleep but when her mind was awake again, she spotted Aidan looking down at her wearing a worried expression on his face.

Frowning, she tried to recollect the last moments and felt bad when she recalled her last thought before she fell asleep. It was remorse which had filled her at the thought of having left her groom behind.

"Aidan. I'm so sorry for having left without anything," she immediately said her voice still hoarse from sleep. "All I remember was that I had to run to save my life."

He nodded but not without Kate noticing the bags under his eyes. "I know Katie. Are you okay now? Are you still feeling the headache?"

She shook her head as she tried to sit up on the bed. "No. I'm fine. I can remember everything now; even what happened after I ran from the murderer. Everything is clearer now." She knew he wanted to ask her about the murderer and she bit her lips trying to figure out what to say. She hoped that she won't disappoint him.

"Do you remember who assaulted you?"

"No," she finally said almost cringing when she saw him grimace. "I was hugging Edward when someone came from behind. He was wearing a mask and a robe which seemed ridiculous to me. I tried to back away from Edward's embrace but then it all happened so quick that I had no time to react."

"He stabbed Edward?" asked Aidan sounding surprised.

"Yes. While he was still hugging me. And I was so shocked. When I saw the knife in his raised hand, I only had the time to shout something but Edward did not even had the time to turn round. He was stabbed in the ribs from behind."

"So he was here to kill Edward?" asked Aidan eagerly.

She knew he wanted her to confirm that the killer was after Edward. It would mean that she was safe but it was not the truth.

"No. He was after me. I did not know it at that time. I tried to hold Edward who was falling down to the floor. My wedding dress was full of blood and when I looked up, I saw him raising the knife in my direction."

"Damn!!! You must have been so scared," put in Aidan and she nodded. If only he knew.

"I was. But mostly I was still trying to figure out what to do. Suddenly I got the presence of mind to throw Edward's body on him."

Aidan laughed dryly. "I bet he wasn't expecting that!"

Kate had to smile back. "No, he wasn't. He was so surprised that he lost his balance and the body fell on him. I did not give him time to react and fled from the fitting room. I cried for help but there was no one in the north wing as everybody was getting ready in the west wing. And Caitlin was fetching some pins from the east wing. There was no time to think as he was fast behind me and I ran outside."

Aidan nodded.

"As it was only minutes before the wedding, the guards were off duty and there was no one to help me. All I knew was that I was running trying to keep my head straight. At some point I stopped and tore my dress because it was preventing me from running in large strides and I threw my plumps away. Then I fell and hurt my head. But I remember that I got up and continued running like a mad person. And when I finally stopped, I had no idea why I was running. It was horrible."

She stopped tears filled her eyes as she remembered the horrible feeling of not knowing anything about her past. Of not even knowing her name. She had felt so lost and forlorn. "I tried to figure out the situation but there was only speculations. I even doubted you but then I found somewhere to hide."

And he knew the rest. She found a convent to hide where he found her. She sighed; it was leading them nowhere even with her memory back. As if reading her mind, he repeated the exact words that had just passed in her mind.

"Yah I agree. I cannot even confirm if it was a male or female. Personally, I would opt for a male. But I'm not even sure of that."

"But you can give at least a hint. A clue or anything you can remember?"

Trying to replay the sequence in her mind, she frowned as she focused on the part where the killer had appeared. He had been covered from head to toe; and it was really difficult for her to discern whether he had been a male or a well-built female.

"Really, I had no time to think. All I know was that when the figure appeared, I frowned at the peculiar costume and tried to disentangle from Edward's arms. The latter had his back towards the newcomer and was oblivious to anyone joining us."

When he did not reply, she went on. "At first I thought somebody was playing a joke. Then when I saw him raising a knife, I cried out to warm Edward but there was really no time to react; he had stabbed

Edward in the ribs. Three times. It happened so quickly that I froze in shock. Then I managed to run from him."

"Damn! This is getting more complicated. I was so hoping on you getting your memory back to finally know who was the murderer."

She frowned. What did he mean? Was there something he was hiding from her? Then she remembered him telling her that the police was suspecting her. "I did not kill him. Hell, I could not kill anyone."

Aidan nodded again wiping his hand across his face in a sign of weariness. "I know. That's what I told you. But the damn local police are fixated on tagging you as the culprit. And I'm afraid that if we go back even now, they will waste time trying to grill you."

"Yah I understand now why you kept me here. No one knows we're here, right?" she asked suddenly afraid that whoever had been trying to kill her might start all over again.

"No, not even your Dad."

She rounded her eyes in surprise. Not even her Dad? Hell! "Why? Are you suspecting him of…"

"Don't be silly. I just thought that the fewer people knew about our whereabouts, the better it would be."

Well, that made sense. "Right. But he must be damned worried about me."

"Oh I phone him every day to update him of the situation. Apart from him, only Ryce knows that I've found you out. Like I told you last time, he's still trying to find a clue with my business enemies but I've got no news of him for the past two days."

"What about my mother and sisters?" asked Kate finally understanding what kind of dilemma she had put everyone into.

"They know nothing. Your father is handling the situation. They are staying at the penthouse since the castle is still under police custody. They said it would take at least one month to clear the area but yesterday your father informed me that the police still had some last moment thing to do before releasing their hold on the castle."

Kate felt bad for her family; it must have been such a difficult phase for them too. "Can I speak to my father?"

"I'm not sure it is a good idea but what the hell! You've already gone through so much already. I guess a few words with your dad won't hurt," he said winking and Kate knew he was just humoring her. It was always like that with Aidan; even if he did not want her to do something he would support her anyway.

It warmed her heart to know that he had not changed his behavior towards her and could not help feeling lucky to have someone like him in her life. Unable to stop herself, she jumped in his arms and laughed when he caught her.

"Thank you. I love you," she said kissing him lightly on the cheeks. She welcomed the familiar feeling of being near him; his exclusive scent sending thrills down her arms like it never failed to. She remembered now how it had always been between them even when she had no idea who he was. She had always been attracted to him; even with no memory of her past.

"Love you too," he replied back instantly giving her a quick peck. "But be careful about what you say. Please. We can never be safe enough," Aidan warned and nuzzled her face tenderly.

Kate readily agreed and the moment she heard her father's voice, she felt like a teenager wanting to squeal with happiness. Damn! She had missed him so much. "Dad?!! How are you?"

"Kate?!!" was the well expected exclamation. "Kate?!!! Is that you?!!!" was the even louder response.

"Yah it's me. I remember everything. Dad, I'm so sorry for..."

"Oh babydoll, you don't have to apologize. I know it has been hard for you too sugar. Tell me about how you're feeling. Are you okay?"

Kate grimaced at Aidan and the latter smiled at her childishness; she knew she had the tendency to behave like a child whenever she was with her father. It was simply because he loved her so much that he made her still feel like a child.

"Dad, I'm fine. I'm okay," she reassured him quickly knowing that he must have been worried out of his mind to have his eldest daughter missing for almost a month now. "I feel better. And I have no idea who killed Edward Bigfoot. He was wearing a ridiculous black robe, gloves and a mask," she blurted out feeling the pressure that everyone had been relying on her to divulge the identity of the murderer.

She repeated the whole story to her father who sighed when she had finished. "This is not helping us at all. The police are still on your trail and I cannot handle your mother anymore. Thankfully, we're getting the castle back next week and we will have to shift again."

"Oh, Dad. I'm so sorry," she apologized feeling down that she had disappointed both Aidan and her father. They had been pinning so much hope on her having her memory back to identify the murderer.

"Don't be sorry sugar. We underestimated the killer. He is a cunning one. I cannot believe someone would try to harm us though. I have never meant harm to anyone. I think the killer was expecting you to be alone and when he found Edward there, he panicked. I feel so sorry for Abigail, she's really aggrieved."

"Poor Edward. He saved my life. Do you think we should get back?"

"Hell, no!" replied her father instantly. "I don't want my daughter in jail; even Uncle Gregory is unable to do anything for us. After the investigation, they found absolutely no clue about the murderer.

Not even until now. So they are assuming that Edward attacked you and you killed him in self-defense."

"Yah so I've heard. But I thought the situation might improve now that I have got my memory back," she said tentatively. Her father was right though. It would be her words and she doubted that the police will let her in peace if they had her.

"Oh doll. I know you miss everybody here but I don't recommend you to come back. At least not until we have some clue about the killer."

Kate sighed. She nodded in response but then realizing that she was on the phone and her father could not see her, she chided herself for being silly. Trying not to let her defeat apparent through her voice, she replied a simple yes and cut the call before she felt even sadder.

Her father was right; they were at a moot point and had no other option than to stay in the cottage until something bigger came up. But they could not hide forever. If someone from the authorities found them out, it would look bad for them since they were acting like culprits.

Kate felt that if she continued like that she would go crazy with the questions tormenting her and she wanted to clear her mind. She no longer wanted to think about what could have happened and what better than shopping to boost back her usual spirit? For any girl, shopping was the best convalescence method ever. After changing into fresh clothes, she joined Aidan in the bedroom and got ready for her expedition.

"I'm going for some fresh air. I need to relax before I go completely crazy," she told Aidan who looked at her in surprise.

"You're going shopping?!!" he exclaimed and Kate in the verge of picking up her bag stopped to stare back at him.

"Yeah," she replied sheepishly as Aidan must have guessed that she was once again using the shopping therapy to remover her stress. "I so need a break and…"

Before she had time to finish her sentence, she found herself being hugged in a bear embrace. Surprised, she looked up at him and he kissed her soundly on the mouth. Out of pure reflex, she responded back still uncomprehending why Aidan was so happy that she was going shopping. It was not that he had been a stingy fiancé but he used to tease her about her ever growing wardrobe especially when she dared mention that she had nothing to wear.

When he ended the kiss, she looked at him questioningly and he grinned looking ten years older instantly. "Welcome back honey. I'm so happy to finally find you back."

Understanding dawned and she knew she had been so tightened up lately to behave like she used to. And now that she was back to being herself, she had regained her confidence and wanted to reassert her personality. By going shopping. It did not make sense but she felt like it was the best idea she had since several decades.

She ginned back at him and smooched him back on the mouth. "Don't worry I won't take more than one hour," she promised.

"Yah yah," he replied not believing her one bit. "Just take your phone with you and call me every fifteen minutes," he said.

"Sure," she replied glad that he was giving her some space. Even if she knew it was difficult for him to let her out of his sight, she needed that time to feel good about herself again. "You need to get some rest too," she caressed his eyes and snatched his iPhone. "Try to sleep. And don't worry I will bring some food for lunch. Don't miss me too much," she said blowing a kiss in the air and made for the door.

Never had the sun seemed brighter and the air feel fresher. She had nothing to buy but she was so content just browsing things and recollecting what she liked. She remembered every single detail. It was good to have her personality and taste back. She even had the time to pick a few gifts for her family in guise of repentance for all she had put them through.

Smiling to herself, she felt happy and lighter to know that she had not killed anyone and still had the love of her life by her side. No matter how hard it was going to be, she knew that eventually everything would be sorted out. She just wished that the killer was not someone she knew and trusted. Lost in her own world, she did not notice the man who spotted her from afar and crossed the street to follow her.

It was only when she felt a hand on her shoulders that she froze fighting back the panic that came back instantly. Memories about the crime swamped her and she felt powerless to run this time. Her happiness was ephemeral and she had been foolish enough to let her guards down. She opened her mouth to scream but nothing came out as panic overtook her senses.

As she turned round to see who had caught up with her, she prayed that she still had a chance to see Aidan one last time before something terrible happened again.

CHAPTER FIFTEEN: HIS PAST MISTAKE

Some things were easier said than done. Aidan could not sleep a wink after Kate left and even if he knew he was getting paranoid, he could not help wondering if he had done a right thing by letting her go alone. Not when there was someone out there thirsty for her blood.

Finally after thirty minutes he gave up on sleep and double checked his mobile. Furious to see no missed calls in his call log and no new messages, he grabbed some money and his car keys from the shelf and headed for the door.

A sense of foreboding overtook him when he dialed Kate's number over and over but she was not answering. Brooklyn was familiar to him but he had no idea where Kate could be. And he was sure that she was not careless to forget calling him.

"Damn!" he exclaimed in frustration heading towards the nearest shopping mall. But the problem with the Kings Plaza shopping center was that it was always full of people and looking for one particular person was like finding a needle in a haystack.

Trying to keep his rationale, Aidan scanned the area like a zombie but as expected Kate was nowhere to be seen. What if something had happened to her? All over again? He did not think he would be able to take it this time. Trying not to think of the worst, he dialed her phone again and nearly sagged with relief when she picked up.

"Kate? Where the hell are you?" he barked knowing he was sounding sharp but the worry was still gnawing at him and till he did not see her, he would not relax.

"Aidan, baby. I'm at the café shop near the shopping mall. I'm sorry I was..."

"Wait right there! I'll be with you in one sec," he ordered already making his way towards the other side of the street. Feeling some life coming back in his body as he spotted her across the street near a coffee shop, he nearly stopped in the middle of the road when he realized she was not alone.

Ryce? What the hell he was doing here? And how had he caught up with them? Aidan galloped towards them and greeted Ryce with a frown.

"How did you find us?" he growled at his friend not very pleased that his cover was not so effective. If Ryce had found them out, it meant that there was a probability that whoever was trying to kill Kate would track them down as easily.

"Hey relax man! When you called me, my iPhone showed me that the call was from Brooklyn. I went to your apartment but it was closed and the guards told me that they haven't seen you in months. So I took a guess that you were staying at the cottage when I found Kate trying to buy the whole shopping mall."

Aidan relaxed a little but he was still not so content that Ryce had found them. It meant they were exposed to more risk and more danger than he had envisaged. "And you?" he asked turning to the innocent looking Kate sipping her coffee latte. "Haven't I told you to call me every thirty minutes? Do you know how scared I was to let you out of my sight?"

"I know," she replied lifting her palm in surrender. "I was so happy to catch up with Ryce that I forgot to call you," she replied sheepishly and Aidan gave up consoling himself that Kate was fine. "I was feeding him with the latest update; about how I got my memory back and what actually happened on the wedding day," she added patting a seat beside her.

She was too cute to resist. His anger evaporating, he joined them for some coffee while Ryce gave him a detailed explanation about how he had tracked down his business rivals but there was absolutely no indication that they had tried to kill him. His best friend even told him that he could not even confirm whether they were aware that he was getting married the idea of his business rival trying to kill Kate to get back at him seemed far-fetched.

Finally, defeated, he had appointed a private detective for the tedious job and he was to be updated every day of any possibility that someone might have something against Aidan or Waldorf Enterprise.

Aidan acknowledged that it did seem ridiculous now that he had found out that Kate had not been kidnapped as he had initially assumed. But he was not ready to leave any stone unturned. Better safe than sorry.

He was almost sure that the killer must have been someone close to them. Someone who meant them harm because of his relationship with Kate. Wasn't it symbolic that the killer had suddenly decided to attack on their wedding day?

"That's okay," he replied Ryce who apologized for not being able to turn up with anything. "Let's keep the PI for some time just to be on the safe side. Alex told us that morning that the police was in the verge of releasing the castle since they had found no other clue. The

Bigfoots have still not withdrawn the case against Kate and that is why we decided to hide some more even with her memory back."

"Yah, I think it's the only way out for the moment. Kate has filled me up with the rest of the story and that was why we did not see you calling up," Ryce informed him and Aidan shrugged still piqued that they had not bothered calling him.

"Never mind," he replied evasively. "Let's focus on the problem at hand. Who can the damned killer be?" he growled. "I think we must make a list of suspects and try to find a motive. I believe that the motive was our love story because the fact that the killer attacked on the wedding day cannot be coincidental."

Kate looked at him puzzled. "Who the hell could have been resentful because we were getting married?"

"That is the question," Ryce intervened putting emphasis on the sentence and both Aidan and Kate looked at him puzzled. "Okay let's start with you," he continued signaling in the direction of Kate. "Try to remember anything you can on the killer. What he was wearing or his approximate height. Anything that could give us a clue. Anything at all."

Kate frowned in concentration and Aidan knew how painful it was for her to remember that nightmare over and over again. "He was wearing a pair of kitchen gloves and the black robe was a bit like that of a lawyer."

At that, both Ryce and Aidan sat up their interest piqued. "Lawyer?" they both asked in chorus looking at each other with a question in their eyes. Aidan raked his mind about who could be a lawyer in either his or Kate's family.

"Are you sure he was a man?" asked Ryce before Aidan could speak out what was in his mind. It did not mean anything anyway. Anybody could rent a lawyer's robe from someone.

Kate shook her head. "I have no guarantee but all I can say was that he or she was well-built and had the more probability of turning out into being a man. As I could not even see his hand, I did not know whether he had hairs or not."

"Hmmm what about Nathalie? She is quite well-built," asked Ryce and Aidan looked back at him shocked. Nathalie Bigfoot?

Would she kill her own brother? Of course he had made a fool out of Nathalie when he had been trying to catch the attention of Kate and she might have avenged herself of being scorned. But was she that desperate to go as far as killing her own brother?

"Nathalie?" squealed Kate looking at Ryce like he had lost his mind. "Why would Nathalie kill Edward?"

"Not Edward. I think Edward's murder was only some collateral damage. She was coming for you," replied Ryce. "Do you remember there was a time Aidan was dating her…"

"I was not dating her. We just had two shopping dates and she only started to flirt with me when she realized I had lots of money," contradicted Aidan indignantly.

"Whatever. You did use her to make Kate jealous. I personally think she waited for a long time before finally avenging herself by spoiling the wedding."

"But Ryce there are ways and ways to spoil a wedding. Not by killing your own brother, damn it!" shouted Kate unable to digest the fact that Nathalie could kill her own brother. Aidan could in a way understand her vehemence to defend Nathalie. It was inhuman to picture someone so evil as to kill her own brother only to avenge her bruised ego. But hell hath no fury like a woman scorned, wasn't that what was said?

"I agree. It does sound a bit far-fetched," Ryce eventually agreed when nobody said anything after a long period of time. " Let's be objective. For a start I don't think your aunts and uncles were responsible. They were already in the church waiting for you to make your appearance."

"How can you be so sure?" asked Aidan frowning. It was possible that a guest had stayed behind and had attempted to kill Kate at the appropriate moment.

"Because I have retrieved the footage from the cameraman who had been taping the guests while waiting for the bride to make her entry. I have ticked every person who was present on the guest list and at the church. There was everyone present even Jade and June the bridesmaid. The only persons missing at the last minute were really close family."

Kate looked back at Aidan ready to deny that it was quite impossible but he managed to keep an impassible face instead of reassuring her. It was what his hunch had been telling him too ever since he had learnt that Kate had been attacked. Because the guards had gone off duty only minutes before the wedding and no one could have made it pass the security cameras.

"Aidan! How can you…" she started to protest when she realized that Aidan was not on her side too. It was not that he was taking sides but he wanted to hear Ryce's version before making up his mind about the whole thing.

So instead of answering, he squeezed her hand and she swallowed hard cutting off whatever she had been trying to say.

"I know," Aidan replied offering a gentle smile. "Let's hear what Ryce has to say."

"Okay," the latter went on relentlessly. It was so typical of Ryce. He was always so focused. Aidan had not thought of asking the cameraman for the footage as he had been too focused on Kate. At that time, he was so glad that he had a friend who had kept his calm through all the drama going on while he had been giving Kate all his attention.

"So the really close family obviously means the parents who were in the west wing getting ready. Judith and Alex were all gathered with the groom along with Meredith – your mother...," he said pointing to Aidan. "... and so they had each an alibi. I exonerate all of them."

Kate let out a sign which was more of frustration than relief. It was clear that she was not at all thinking along the same lines.

Ignoring her, Ryce went on. "As for Caitlin, she was with you trying to fix your dress and I don't think she would have left you to mask herself and then come back to kill you. So I exclude her also."

"Thank you," muttered Kate in a somewhat ironical voice and Aidan squeezed her hand again. They had to be objective. They could not exclude anyone without going into full details.

"But I'm not saying that she's completely off the hook. She was the only one without an alibi. Nathalie was also in the west wing but nobody saw her. Not even her mother who was also gathered in the hall with the groom."

"What do you mean? Do you think Caitlin could have killed me?! What about the fact that she's petite and could not have fitted that robe?" shouted Kate angrily.

"Kate, will you relax?" Aidan intervened. He knew that she was very sensitive about her family but Ryce was right. They had to analyse the situation rationally without letting emotions getting the better of them else it would lead them nowhere.

Kate sighed sadly and nodded sagging her shoulders in defeat. "I think you're right."

"What?!!" queried Aidan stunned. He would never have expected her to agree that one of her family members or someone close to her could have betrayed her. Kate had always been so optimistic and it was so hard to have her face the true nature of life so brutally. "Do you know anything else?' he asked not voicing out his concern as it would deter her.

She gave him a small casual shrug but the defensive gesture portrayed so much hurt that it broke his heart. He was not happy that Kate was in so much pain.

"When I tried to flee, the killer seemed to know his way round the house. And since the castle was so big, I could bet my life that the killer was as familiar with the castle as I am. But I will never accept the fact that Caitlin could be my attacker," she protested vehemently.

Ryce nodded. "In fact I'm telling you my trail before we talked. I had made a list of suspects long before I knew anything about the murder. I have revised my list when you have described the killer. That is why I eliminated Caitlin. Bryan was with the kids getting them ready and I don't think he would have left them alone. So it leaves us with only…Nathalie," he concluded looking at them with a frown.

Aidan knew there was something else he was not telling them. "What?" he snapped impatiently. It was better if everything was out now so that they could decide in which direction to go.

"There is also Jennifer who certified she was with a sleeping Flint in our room but there was no witness," he stated matter-of-factly but Aidan knew how much it must have cost him to give them that piece of information.

"She's not so well-built too," replied Kate in a small voice and Aidan knew it was hurting her to be doubting her own people. But if Ryce was not exonerating Jennifer, it surely meant he was keeping his objectivity.

"I agree. So we eliminate Jen and therefore we have only one culprit. Nathalie," announced Ryce and Kate looked at him with something akin to hope in her golden eyes.

Aidan did not know what to make of the information. Nathalie Bigfoot was a spoilt and rude woman but that hardly qualified her as a murderer. Hasn't she once told him that she loved her brother very much and the Thorntons had known her for years.

Could there be a murderer under her pretty face? It was hard to picture her as a revengeful person but he was damn sure that the fact that the attacker had struck on their wedding day meant something. Someone was not happy with their relationship and was trying to make a statement; an obvious statement.

Ryce and Kate chatted about possibilities about how to handle the "Nathalie" situation sure that she was the culprit. Aidan was silent assimilating the situation and mentally exploring other possibilities. Since the prime suspects were Nathalie, Jennifer and Caitlin in that particular order, he was trying to look for a motive for the murder attempt.

Personally he was pretty sure that it could not be Nathalie since her own brother had been murdered. In the worst case scenario, if she had come to kill Kate and found her brother there, she would have hit him or something instead of assassinating him.

So the question was whether it was Jennifer or Caitlin. However he tried, he could not find a motive for Caitlin to try to kill her own sister. They were so close anyway that it was hard to picture sweet Caitlin as a murdered.

That meant he was left with only Jennifer Avery Calhoun. But he was wise enough not to voice it out in front of Ryce.

Would he believe that Jen was a killer? Was that why she had fled before anyone could question her? Aidan had not bothered to check whether Flint had been really sick or if it was an excuse. He had not been thinking straight at that time. But Ryce would know if Jen had been feigning the sickness of her own child.

He opened his mouth to ask him just that when another thought hit him like a whirlwind.

Wait a second. Wait a bloody second. Everybody fitted the scenario. They had covered the track of each and every one. Except one. What if the killer was clever enough to turn the attention to someone else? While he and Kate would be busy investigating on someone else, the real cunning murderer would be free to complete his task.

While they had covered every track, every past movement of the family, they had forgotten about Ryce. Where the hell was Ryce when everything was going on? He had not mentioned himself at all in the scenario and Aidan was sure he was not with them in the hall. Not until it had been announced that the bride had disappeared.

It gave him ample time to do whatever he had to do. Then Aidan chided himself for being silly. Why the hell was he doubting Ryce, his best friend? The one who was helping him solving the puzzle? But the more Aidan thought about it, the more he seemed to doubt that it could be Nathalie. And neither Caitlin. If it was Jennifer, then there was no way she could have done that hideous task alone.

What if Ryce was in cahoots with Jen? As far as he knew him personally, Ryce could never do such a thing but there was no one else who was eligible to be a murderer, really. But he could not ignore the fact that there was somebody dead in the castle and therefore a murderer was roaming freely out there. And they have not been in contact for more than six years which was more than enough time for somebody to change completely.

Was that why Ryce had been tracking them down so desperately? Was that why he had joined Kate when he had spotted her? Had he been trying to take advantage of her memory loss to trap her? Because Ryce had no idea that Kate had gotten back her memory. And after Kate had recognized him, he must have thought about his action and could hardly attack her in a public place.

Had his premonitions been right? What would have happened if he had not joined them quickly? Would Ryce have attempted something else? But Aidan doubted he would have killed her without a plan. The killer whoever it was very very meticulous and would not have acted impulsively. The more he thought about it, the more he found that the murderer matched the personality of Ryce.

Meticulous. Focused. Cunning. Ryce Vin Connor. But why the hell would Ryce try to kill Kate? Then he knew.

What if they had never forgiven him for the past? For having betrayed Jennifer like he had done on their graduation night. What if every professed words of friendship had been a lie? A ruse to get what they had wanted all along? Because who knew better than them that his weak link was Kate. Is she was no more, he would be finished.

Aidan had to bite his tongue to stop himself from letting the words out of his mouth. Would Ryce be so evil as to try to kill Kate to get even for what had happened in the past?

CHAPTER SIXTEEN: INNOCENT UNTIL PROVEN GUILTY

"Can you believe it's Nathalie?" Kate asked as soon as they reached back the cottage. She knew she had her moment of reprieve and that Aidan would never let her out of his sight again. But the shopping trip had done her a lot of good and she was happy to have met Ryce.

"I don't know what to think anymore," replied Aidan enigmatically. "Let's forget about that for a moment."

"Hmmm what else did you have in mind?" she asked coquettishly glad that Ryce had declined her offer to stay at the cottage. Not that the latter had actually declined but Aidan had quickly pointed out that they would be exposed to more risks if Ryce disappeared too.

When Aidan smiled at her suggestive comment, she grinned back wanting to let go of all their worries for a moment. It had been so long since she had been happy and carefree. Like she had always been. How she had missed him. And the moments they had spent together. But in the turmoil, they had not even taken the time to reunite properly.

It was no wonder with so many things going on around them. She had been so happy to finally become Mrs. Waldorf only to have her dreams shattered at the last minute. And suddenly she knew what she wanted most.

"Let's get married," she stated impulsively and Aidan stared at her unbelievably.

"What?! Are you out of your mind? I had something else in mind. Something more like this," he said and grabbing her in his arms to rain light kisses on her neck where she was ticklish. She giggled trying to get away but he blocked her escape by tightening his hold on her.

When finally, she was able to free herself for some air, she punched him lightly in the ribs. "I'm serious. Let's get married. I don't care about anything or anyone else right now."

"But you've always wanted a grand wedding, remember?" Aidan reminded her smoothly apparently not taking her seriously. She knew he would never believe that Kate Thornton would dare get married without her beloved family around. But she had reached a point where she could tolerate it no more.

It had been years and years since she had loved Aidan and she wanted to be his. Officially. Legally. And completely. No matter what.

"I've already had two grand weddings which are enough to last me a lifetime," she reminded him with a grimace at the mention of her two previous wedding fiascos. Seriously, she had always believed in fairy-tale weddings but she had enough of organizing weddings and not getting married. Especially when she had been sure of wanting to be Mrs. Aidan Waldorf for the past eight years. "This time I sincerely don't care about anything else."

He seemed a bit taken aback at her latest statement and pulled her back to look at her more closely. "You can't be serious!" It was more a statement than a question and she sighed.

"I am. All I've ever wanted to be is your bride and whoever is trying to stop us will not win so easily. If the fact that I'm getting married to you killed poor Edward and put my family in such a trauma, I want them defeated."

"B…but what about your family?" stammered Aidan apparently really surprised that she could come up with such an idea and that too in such a complicated situation. Well, she had and she still did. It would be what she wanted in any situation anyway.

"I don't care. They will have to understand. Listen, if we get married, then if Nathalie had tried to kill me, she will lose. And maybe she will stop whatever madness had gotten into her."

It made sense, didn't it? If the killer wanted to stop their wedding, there was nothing he would be able to do when the deed was done.

"So you're marrying me to avenge the killer?" he said and Kate threw him a quick look to see whether he was serious or not. Thankfully, he winked at her and Kate realized he had only been teasing her.

"The more I think about it, I have this feeling that it must be Nathalie," she continued. "I can't even envisage that she might have killed her brother though. All I can think to justify such an act was that she must have been high on something at that time."

"Why? Did you see the killer act in a weird way or something?" asked Aidan puzzled.

"No," she replied in a small voice. "But I can see no other explanation. Can you?" she asked looking up at him and by the look of his face she realized that he was hiding something from her.

"What is it?" she asked feeling weird. It was like having a premonition that whatever was going to come her way was something very very bad and that she might not like it a bit. But she had to know. She was done with being always in the dark and the last to know what was happening. "Please tell me," she practically begged.

"I don't think it's Nathalie. If you say she was high or something she would never had the presence of mind to return back to normal after having killed her own brother. She would have been hysterical but on the contrary our killer was so normal that we have not a single clue who he could be."

Kate nodded. He was right of course. It was just a hypothesis anyway as she had no other explanation. And ever since Ryce had planted the seed of doubt in her head, it was difficult to remove it.

"I guess you're right. Ever since I got the idea that Nathalie could be the murderer, it's difficult for me to picture someone else."

"Exactly!" he exclaimed so suddenly that Kate nearly jumped. Why was he so vehement all of a sudden? "What if it had been a ploy all along? What if it was Ryce the murderer and he is trying to mislead us?"

Kate felt shock swamp her and her first reaction was to deny such a possibility. "Aidan! Are you out of your mind? Why would Ryce try to kill me? I have done nothing to him that he could hate me so much!"

"Right! I mean you have done nothing to anybody anyway. Hell, you of all person don't deserve to die but not everybody is on the same wavelength as us. Somebody is evil enough to consider you as a menace or burden. And want you gone."

At his words, she felt a feeling of depression in her heart. It was as if her small world had come crumpling down. She had always believed that she was an exceptionally good person and that the people around her loved her very much. But she realized now that it was only an illusion. Aidan was right. Somebody hated her so much that he wanted her dead.

"Are you sure it's Ryce?" she croaked feebly no longer wanting to live in her cocoon of safety where she gave everybody the benefit of doubt.

"I'm not hundred percent sure but remember while he was analyzing the situation, he never once mentioned where he was. And he even incriminated Jennifer so that we would believe his objectivity. But what if they were in cahoots?"

"Ryce and Jen?" she muttered feeling her jaw as heavy as if someone had filled it with lead. She wanted to cry. Howl most probably. Her two best friends wanted to kill her?

Even if she did not deserve that, it was life and nobody said that life was fair. But she could not understand why Ryce would want her dead. It was simply heart-breaking. She knew where Aidan was getting at.

"Yes," Aidan answered and the eerie way he said the monosyllable sent shivers down her spine. "I believe they're in this together." He paused before looking at her with a sad expression in his eyes. "For making us pay for what happened in the past."

Damn! It was what she had suspected. Of course, they wanted to get back for the past. She had been the one responsible for breaking Jennifer and Aidan. But she had thought that they had moved on with that story. They had gotten married and they had a child together. Wasn't that enough to forget past mistakes and move on?

"Do you think she still loves you and that she had been acting all along? That they never got married and that Flint is not even their child? Do you think they would go to such extremes to hurt us? I mean we did hurt them but if they wanted revenge, why kill me?"

Aidan nodded. "I have been thinking about that too. Maybe he had not meant to kill you or Edward. Maybe he was only trying to scare the hell out of you so that you'd freak out enough to cancel the wedding and Edward got accidently murdered."

Kate pondered on the new theory trying to match it with what had actually happened. When she saw the funny persona entering the fitting room, she could not gauge the reaction of whether the person was shocked to find Edward there because of the mask hiding the face. But she knew that he had stabbed Edward mercilessly and without any second thoughts.

When Edward had wriggled in pain, the killer had stabbed him twice more which meant that he had not only wanted to hurt him but he was here to kill.

"No, I can vouch for the fact that whoever it had been had the time to knock Edward off if he had wanted to. Because the latter had his back to him and was in no position to defend himself. So, the killer wanted no witness around."

Aidan sighed. And Kate knew that he had been hoping that they would finally get somewhere. "Personally, I think Nathalie was in love with you. And she tried to kill me but was surprised to find Edward there. She killed her brother too to mask her cover because she knew nobody would doubt her if Edward was killed."

"Maybe you are right. I frankly don't know what to think. I will hire a private detective to put after Nathalie but let me warn you if she is clear then I am damned sure it's Ryce and Jennifer. Except I'm not sure whether they're in this together."

"I can't believe it's Jennifer. If ever Jennifer had been lying about Flint, I would have known. You remember I was the one who brought him from Aunt Helen. I don't think she would participate in such a devious act. Unless she had no idea..."

Her voice faltered. Aunt Helen was the mother of Jennifer and they were quite fond of her. During their university days, they had often stayed over at her house since she lived in Brooklyn and could not imagine that she could dupe them into believing that Flint was not her grandson.

When Jen and Ryce had attended her first wedding, they had not revealed the fact that they were married at first as they were not in good terms. And when they had finally revealed their linked past, Kate had asked her father to bring little Flint in guise of repentance for what she had done in the past.

"Hmmm," acknowledged Aidan his forehead creasing in concentration. "That would mean that Flint is their son because there's no way Aunt Helen would participate in their charade. And if they had a child together, there was no way they could still hold such a grudge against us."

"I think it's Nathalie. I never got along with her anyway. She must have fallen in love with you along the way and must have waited for the right moment to attack me."

"Okay, let me make some calls. I think it would be better to hire two detectives; one after Nathalie and the other after Jennifer. I frankly do not know who to suspect anymore. And everybody is innocent until proven guilty."

Kate made another grimace at his words. He was right. They could hardly blame anyone unless they were sure. And since they both had a different opinion, it was better to find some more clues before starting in a specific direction.

After Aidan had talked to his secretary, Kate felt sad and wanted to forget all her worries. But she knew that if it was by any chance Ryce who had tried to attack them, it meant that she was not safe at the cottage anymore.

"Do you think we should go somewhere else? I mean if you believe that Ryce is the killer, he might attack again tonight?"

Aidan looked at her pensively. It was clear that he had not thought in that perspective and when he pinched his forehead, Kate knew he was having a headache. And she felt bad for him. Maybe she was worrying needlessly.

"I'm sorry..."she began and stopped when Aidan shook her head.

"No, you're right. I should have thought of it. I'm the one who should be sorry. I have not been thinking with a clear head lately. I so don't want the killer to be Ryce," he finally said in a groggy voice which arouse whenever he got emotional.

Kate realized how he was counting on the fact that Ryce was not the killer. Aidan loved him as much as his own brother and if ever it was Ryce the killer, Aidan would be heart-broken. And so would she. For their own well-being, Kate hoped fiercely that Ryce and Jen had nothing to do with what had happened on her wedding day.

Talking of wedding days, she was so fed up with them that she no longer had the courage to get married grandly again. "Let me pack my bags and we can leave. I think we should stay in a hotel far from Brooklyn so that Ryce cannot trace us again. But before I want us to take our vows."

"No, not now. This is so not the right moment," replied Aidan instantly and Kate frowned at him angrily.

"Just bring a minister and two witnesses. So that we can have a quiet ceremony. And I don't care what happens after that," she said feeling forlorn like she had been before her shopping trip.

She knew it was not the moment nor the time. But if she had to die, she would rather die as his wife now. It was the only thing that had remained rock solid in her toughest times and she did not want to let go of that.

"Please," she insisted. And Aidan nodded resignedly pinching his phone again.

At that precise moment, she promised to herself that no matter what happened, she vowed to herself that no harm would come to Aidan or the rest of her family. If the killer had something against her, she would be the sacrificial lamb and making sure nobody else got hurt.

She had had enough of everybody trying to protect her. This time she would be the strong one and whoever was trying to kill her would not win so easily.

"Right, by that time I will be packed and done."

"What about your dress? What are you going to wear?" Aidan asked and Kate saw it as an effort to deter her from getting married than anything else. What did it matter what she wore anyway? She'd had two wedding dresses and she was not very keen to dress up as a bride again.

So, she shrugged. "I'll find something."

Aidan shook his head looking at her in amazement.

"What?" she asked suddenly self-conscious.

"You will never stop to amaze me. You are the most wonderful woman on this earth and I'm so lucky to have you," he said hugging her close. "I have called a friend for the minister and he's joining us with another friend."

"Fine, I'll run and refresh myself," she said thrilled that she was finally going to be Mrs. Waldorf. It was unexpected that Aidan had agreed to get married but with everything going on, she was never sure of what could happen next.

Feeling happy, she chose a plain ivory coloured dress which was in the luggage Aidan had brought her the first day they had been in the cottage. When she wore it, it landed inches below her knees. Unfortunately she had no hair drier and her wet hair was not very stylish. Trying her best, she finally gave up putting some of Aidan's gel to give her hair the wet look. It looked pretty decent when she was done.

Thankfully, she had brought some make up while she had been shopping and when she looked at herself in the mirror, she found some of her initial glow coming back. It was after some three months that she had made herself pretty and she was liking it.

When she came downstairs, Aidan dressed in a classy tuxedo was already waiting for her along with three strangers. One was the minister, she guessed by his attire and the others was the close friends he had mentioned. She was introduced to the two friends who apparently knew Aidan when he was doing his MBA.

"Nice to meet you Luke," she smiled to the second friend. The other friend Jordan was busy with some papers and Kate knew Aidan must have asked him to get the license which had been ready since so long. The original wedding seemed so long ago now.

Her attention snapped back when the minister started his usual summons. And it finally seeped in that she was going to be Mrs. Aidan Waldorf. And her heart filled with so much happiness that she felt all her past pain fade. Whoever was trying to kill her had lost and she was still alive and with the man of her dreams.

Smiling till it hurt, she concentrated on the words which floated in the air. Especially when the minister asked Aidan to tell his vows. Her handsome groom looked at her with love shining in his eyes and Kate could not help feeling lucky.

"I, Aidan Flint Waldorf, take you, Katherine Iris Thornton to be my wife. I promise to be true to you in good times and in bad, in sickness and in health. I will love you and honor you all the days of my life until death do us apart."

Kate felt sure her face glowed with happiness and she smiled back at him repeating the wedding vows. And the sweet words followed. "You have declared your consent. May the Lord in his goodness strengthen your consent and fill you both with his blessings. What God has joined, men must not divide. I declare you man and wife. You may now kiss the bride."

As Aidan bent to kiss her, Kate closed her eyes to savor her first kiss as his bride. It was such a wonderful moment when his lips touched hers tentatively at first and then his tongue started to probe its entry in her mouth.

Pouring every feeling blossoming in her heart, she responded to his each demand. "I love you," she whispered when he broke off the kiss. And he kissed her lightly again.

"I love you too. Forever and ever."

Both were so engrossed in each other that they missed what was happening around them. They never noticed the cars pulling up in the driveway. They never saw anyone moving towards them until it was too late.

"Katherine Iris Thornton! How dare you?"

CHAPTER SEVENTEEN: THE SURPRISE VISIT

Surprised to hear the furious outburst behind him, Aidan whirled around and stood in front of Kate to protect her out of sheer reflex. And he found himself facing a fuming Judith Thornton. Aw hell! Her timing sucked as usual.

His new mother-in-law stood two feet away looking down at them with an angry and menacing expression. And as if it was not enough, the whole family stood behind her looking a bit less angry but somewhat stunned. In the heat of the moment, he completely forgot their dangerous situation and his heart constricted at the thought of the encounter between mother and daughter that would follow.

It was simply not fair. Kate had decided to be selfish once in her entire life only to be immediately admonished. As if they had not suffered long enough. It had been three months since the wedding fiasco and they had not a moment of reprieve ever since.

Even if inappropriate, he had understood her urgency to get married at such a delicate time of their life. While he had not completely agreed with her, it had been difficult for him to refuse her request. He simply had not the heart to say no to her especially with the type of events in queue where they were never sure what could happen next. Ultimately, he had relented to her demand and his as well despite all his misgivings; it was better for them to finally belong to each other and whatever came their way would have to wait.

Thankfully, he had every papers with him and it had been not difficult to arrange for the preparations. Amazed was a weak word to describe how he felt when Kate had refused any frivolities and extravagance. While he had expected her to complain and want at least a decent wedding like any other woman, she had taken the situation sportingly. It would seem that the most important thing to her was becoming his bride and that fact had touched him deeply.

It had made him realize how lucky he was to have such a wonderful woman by his side. It had been the most wonderful moment of his life when they had shared their vows. He had finally acquiesced that it was what he had wanted all along too. Only to be interrupted by a red-faced fiercely looking Judith to spoil their oomph moment.

"Mom…" Kate was saying in a warning tone.

But Judith being Judith ignored her warning and lashed out mercilessly about how could her eldest daughter get married without informing her family. Aidan cringed at her lack of tack and looked at Alex for help. Not so surprisingly, Alex was grinning widely completely ignoring his wife's outburst and opened his arms at his daughter.

Kate picking up the cue ignored her mother too and jumped in her father's arms for a big bear hug. "Oh Kate. I'm so happy for you," he said huskily with a trace of tears in his voice.

"Thanks Dad! It's been so long; I have missed you. How are you?"

On seeing the father-daughter reunion, Judith seemed to overcome the shock and realize her mistake. Putting a stop to her unnerving rant, she smiled at Kate too and they both hugged making peace.

"I'm sorry honey. I know my outburst was uncalled for but I have missed you so much. And imagine my shock seeing you getting married in such a … dress," Judith remarked looking at Kate's outfit in disgust and Aidan mentally slapped his forehead.

Women! Even in the worst situations, all they could think of was clothes, clothes and clothes. But he was glad to see Kate smiling even if it was a wobbly kind of smile. If Kate was happy then it meant that everything was fine.

Then suddenly, he remembered one thing. Who could have informed the whole family of their whereabouts? And only minutes before they were going to leave? It had to be Ryce since he was the only one who had traced them in the morning.

Damn! That meant his doubts were confirmed. Sending his friend a look which spoke volume, he immediately went on his guard. Now that they had been discovered, he was ready to face anything. Ryce seemed to pick his signal and sent him a look which gave him the impression that the latter had been desperate but he was not buying it. Not this time.

"Why are you here, anyway?" Kate was asking after hugging everyone one by one. Aidan knew it was not meant as a reproach because she looked very happy that her family was with her on her special day. But he knew she was also prepared for the worst now.

It was hard for him to guess who the killer could be; or if he was really from her close family as they had assumed? Jade and June looked almost close to tears as Kate held their hands not wanting to let them go. Caitlin and Bryan were snuggled in each other's arms smiling happily their eyes moist with happiness.

Surprisingly, Jennifer had arrived with the family and was standing a few miles away sending furtive looks to Ryce. Like they had something to hide. So it would seem that the only ones who were acting suspicious were his best friends; Ryce and Jennifer. Wasn't it such a coincidence for Jen to finally appear at the right moment?

What if Ryce had told her that he had found Kate out and she had returned immediately to finish her pending task? He felt bad about doubting his own friends but they had a very plausible reason to do such a vile act. Not that it was plausible. But according to them, it would be the ultimate revenge. It was weird that Kate had been separated from her family on her wedding day and had reunited with them on her next wedding day.

"Oh it was all my fault," Judith answered Kate's question. "I overheard Ryce telling Jen that he had found you out and that you were safe and sound. And when I confronted them, they told me everything. But I had so not been expecting you to find you exchanging your vows."

Aidan felt shock in his system; so he had been right! Ryce had not been that objective as he had first pretended to be. If he had suspected Jennifer as he had stated, he would not have informed her about their whereabouts especially when Aidan had prevented him from doing so.

"Judith, I think you should understand that under the circumstances, the kids had no other choice," Alex said still smiling. "It's been three months and Kate is not even allowed to come back to her own house. I think getting married without informing you is not the real problem here," he admonished gently.

Thankfully, Aidan's friends had retreated with the minister in tow and were not present to witness such an awkward family moment. "I know Alex but..."

"Mom, relax!" said Jade. "We're seeing Kate after three months and you should stop your raving. Kate how have you been? Dad told us the whole story. Are you alright?"

Aidan stood watching as Kate related some part of the story to her sisters and Jennifer included but she glanced at him every now and then. He knew she was also worried about the killer getting every information but she could hardly not talk to her sisters.

"I was sure that you were not capable of such an act Kate," Caitlin was saying. If she was the killer then it was either she was a damned good actress or Aidan was a complete fool. There was no way that someone could feign such caring. "But it was so difficult for us, you know," she went on. "Bryan here was always looking out for you. But when we got no news after such a long time, we were all certain that something terrible must have happened to you."

"We were so engrossed in our own problems though," added June looking like she might burst into tears any time.

"Yes, we were out of our own house. And on top if that Nathalie was harassing us all the time by sending the police to interrogate each one of us over and over again," added Jade.

Aidan threw a look at Alex for confirmation and the latter nodded. He had not known of the difficulties that the family had faced at the other end and he regretted the fact that he had not been more considerate to inquire about them. Whenever he had called, it had been to give information about Kate and had been very brief conversations.

Kate looked as depressed as he felt. "I don't blame them," mused Judith. "Abigail and I have become very distant; we don't have the same equation now and I don't think it will be same again. I just wish that things were different and we finally get to know who the culprit is."

"We will," Alex said in an assertive voice. "But I'm afraid that Kate will have to return home now since most of us have found her out. It would be too risky for her to stay here. I have talked to Greg; they will interrogate you. It's inevitable. But they will not imprison you; you will be forbidden to leave the country."

"Do you have any idea who could have attacked you Kate?" Jennifer spoke for the first time and Aidan narrowed his eyes at her. Why would she ask such a question? Was she suddenly afraid that they might have discovered something about the killer? About her?

"Why do you say that?" asked Aidan quickly before Kate could answer. He did not want his bride to disclose how far they were from the truth. He wanted the killer to be on guard too so that he might make a mistake.

Jennifer looked at him uncomprehendingly trying to decipher if he had a hidden meaning in interrupting her so promptly. But he kept his face emotionless and Jennifer shrugged looking somewhat out of her usual calm demeanor. The way they were behaving, it was difficult not to doubt them.

"I don't know. I have talked to Ryce and we still haven't found anything about who could have done such a vile thing."

"Oh, I think I have a pretty good idea who is the killer," announced Kate suddenly and everybody froze to look in her direction, including himself.

What the hell was she playing at? Where the hell had this come from? While they had analyzed who the killer could have been, she had never once mentioned that she had any clue who the killer might be. He looked at her with hooded eyes but she royally ignored him and faced Jennifer with a challenge.

And Aidan finally understood what she was trying to do. She was trying to get the upper hand on them. If she said something about knowing who the killer was, the latter might panic and might do something he had not planned. For he was sure the killer had no intention to attack in front of the whole family looking.

Whoever was responsible for the crime had been very careful to hide his identity. He would not be careless now. But Aidan was furious with Kate for making herself the bait and that too without consulting him.

"You do?" echoed her three sisters at the same time.

Jennifer looked like she had gone yellow in color and Ryce frowned at Kate. He was becoming more and more certain that they were the real culprits. They were behaving so weirdly and did not look so happy to learn the truth that the killer had been identified.

"Well, tell us who it is," said Bryan. "We will hand him over to the police and you have nothing to fear since we are all here with you."

Kate shook her head. "I'd rather talk to the police first."

"What?!" exclaimed Ryce. "Are you sure they're gonna believe you? From what I have gathered, they are hell-bent into believing that you are the killer and I'm afraid that they might turn it into something against you if you don't have any proof."

How clever of him. Ryce wanted to know if Kate had any proofs against him so that he could destroy them before they had time to hand them over to the police. How very very cunning of him. The suspense was starting to get on his nerves.

Aidan had had enough; he so wanted to confront them. It was too late to back out now anyway. But he did not want to put Kate in danger. What if they were found out when they were away from civilization and they realized that their game was over? It would be more difficult for him to protect each member of the family then.

"I think it would be better if we talked to the police directly," he intervened knowing that Kate had no name and worried that they might be found out. "They are going to do their job according to the statement that Kate would give."

"But I don't understand!" protested Ryce. "She told me she had no idea who the killer was. Have you remembered something else? Why the hell are you being so mysterious? Why not tell us who has killed Edward; who is behind all... this?"

"I will. But all in due time. I cannot reveal his name on front of everyone as some person I care for might get hurt. I'd rather wait until..."

"Oh yeah?" exclaimed a voice suddenly from behind the group and they all turned back to see who was the newcomer.

There stood a red faced Nathalie Bigfoot. Closely followed by Abigail Bigfoot. Hell! And she looked furious like the devil had possessed her. It was going to become ugly now, Aidan was sure of that. In an attempt to protect his bride, he got closer to her and the newcomer seemed to notice the subtle movement.

Her eyes got bigger if that was possible and she burst into a tantrum.

"You bitch! You cunning bitch!" she spat her voice full of venom. "Look at how many people are around to protect you. You act like you are the kindness reincarnated when in fact you are nothing but a hypocrite!"

"Nathalie!" reprimanded Judith in an attempt to protect her daughter but the infuriated tramp was beyond consolation. She stood hands on hips looking like she wanted to throw herself on Kate and hit her or something.

"Don't Mrs. Thornton!" she warned and Aidan saw her lifting her hand to stop his mother-in-law from uttering another word. "It is because of her that I lost my brother!"

"You know it's not true!" Aidan defended on seeing the stricken look on Kate's face. Damn! Damn! Damn! He wished he had been cunning enough to protect her from all that drama. "Whoever had killed Edward wanted to kill Kate too!"

And all that happened because Ryce could not hold his tongue long enough. He felt furious with his friend for putting him in such a situation unless it was what his best friend had wanted after all. What if Ryce had purposely disclose their whereabouts because he had wanted to make them weak so that he might attack again?

"Yes and my poor brother was only collateral damage, right?" continued Nathalie in a voice laced with spite. "And if she was so innocent and pious like she always proclaimed herself to be, why the hell is she in hiding? Why the hell had she been hiding for two whole months even after getting her memory back?"

"How do you know that?" asked Aidan wanting her to stop her cruel words because by the look of it, they were having the desired effect on his bride who looked as white as a ghost. With her hand at her throat as she absorbed the words from the evil woman, Aidan knew she was doing herself a great harm by believing the venom being spat at her.

"I hired someone to watch your family closely. When Ryce told your mother that you were with Aidan in Brooklyn, he followed the cars till here. And I got here as soon as I could. Only to hear that…that bitch saying that she knew who killed my brother. Only to be keep her mouth shut after three whole months?"

"Nathalie, you need to calm down," intervened Alex looking at Kate. The latter stood transfixed in shock looking like she might burst into tears any minute now. It was painful to see her grieving so much for something she had not been responsible of. "I was the one who asked Kate to stay back because I was afraid the police might apprehend her as soon as she got back. Besides, she got back her memory and it was not her the killer."

"How do you know that?" asked Nathalie crossing her hands around her chest, the movement showing that she was not ready to give up on her point.

"Well, she remembered everything. And she knows who is the killer. Except that she won't tell anyone except the police. And knowing my daughter, she must be having a good reason for that as well."

"I'm sure," she scoffed. "I want to know who killed my brother. If she knows something let her speak now!"

"Yes," added the mother of the victim. Abigail had spoken for the first time since they got here. "I too wish to know who killed my son," she said in an almost pleading tone looking at Kate with a desperation which would have touched any soul.

"I...," began Kate but she was unable to finish her sentence as she choked back on her tears. It was clear that the accusations being thrown have affected her even if they were uncalled for. She had always been such a sensitive soul and any harsh words affected her deeply.

Not knowing what to say, she swallowed her words and bent her head and Aidan could no longer make out whether it was in defeat or shame. Unfortunately, anybody could get the wrong impression by her stance; it was almost like she was condemning herself.

"You know what I think?" Nathalie said nastily gaining advantage on the situation. "She killed Edward and is concocting a false story to get herself out of the hook. For all we know, it's only her words and I don't believe her."

Alarmed at the turn of the situation, Aidan tried to think of something quickly in case her bluff was found out. Apart from him, nobody else knew that Kate had been lying. But before he could utter another word, somebody else beat him to it.

"Nathalie, Kate is telling the truth," Ryce defended quickly before he had time to think of anything to convince the latter of their bluff. "We know who the killer is but we cannot say his name now. It is too dangerous."

"Oh? And why is that?"

There was an almost ominous silence as everybody stood still and Ryce finally said. "Because he's among us right now."

The silence which followed was eerier and Aidan felt cold settled down in his bones. Nobody said anything each one analyzing the statement. Was Ryce going to confess that he was the murderer? Had he been having qualms about what he had done and he wanted to repent now?

And suddenly amidst the pandemonium, Aidan realized something. Kate was missing. Where the hell had she disappeared now? She had been standing in her place a few minutes ago and now she was no longer in his sight of vision. Where the hell was she?

CHAPTER EIGHTEEN: DANGER AHEAD

It had been Kate's undoing. The look that Aunt Abigail had sent her had touched her deeply. It had been the look of a desperate mother who had just lost her only son and wanted something from her. Something she could not give simply because she did not know the truth.

Feeling forlorn, she felt tears prick her eyes as she stepped back in an attempt to avoid the question being addressed to her. She stammered something unintelligible not knowing what to say. The plain truth was that she had no idea who the killer was and had only been bluffing.

Aidan and Ryce had known she had been faking it and they had protected her. Like they had always done. The killer could not be Ryce; it was simply not possible. Her heart would never believe that.

Even if he had wanted revenge, he would have attempted to harm her in a different way. Ryce would never try to kill her; it was unthinkable.

All her instincts were telling her that it could be Nathalie since the hate she harbored for her was so intense that it was evident even from a distance. But was it enough for a scorned woman to try to kill her? Or kill her brother in the process? The words the latter had spat at her had been laced with hatred even if Kate knew Nathalie had only been trying to break her.

But the words that Nathalie had lashed at her had affected her anyway. No matter what her protectors said, she knew she was the one responsible for the death of Edward. Deeply wounded, she finally acknowledged that she had been living in a cocoon till now always being protected by her loved ones while she was not that innocent like she had believed herself to be.

It was a revelation to her and she had wanted some time alone to face herself. Kate knew she was not supposed to stay alone especially after Aidan had warned her that the killer could be anyone now. But her mind had been too full of remorse for any rational thinking and she backed off silently while everybody had been busy trying to convince Nathalie that she had nothing to do with the actual murder.

But they were wrong. She might not have stabbed that knife but she was as responsible as the killer. Had Edward not been at the wrong place at the wrong time, he would have still been alive. And she felt bad for having been able to escape while he was dead. All because of her. She should have at least protected him but the fact was that she had no time to react. It had happened so suddenly that her first instinct had been to save herself.

Not for one second had she stopped to think of poor Edward lying wounded on the floor. Was she selfish? It was human nature to love oneself more than others she knew but now she was feeling so bad. Except that if she had stayed back, she would not have been able to save Edward as she would have been dead by now.

But like Nathalie said, it was only her words that were going to testify her innocence. She had no other way to convince anyone that she had only been following her instinct. It was what anyone would have done in her place but had it been her brother who had landed dead, she would have reacted in the same way too.

Finally realizing that she was walking without destination, she stopped walking and focused on her whereabouts. Her famous headache was back after a long time and she sat on the side of a fountain staring blindly at the way the water was splashing. It was so depressing to have finally faced the two Bigfoots. She now understood why Aidan was so reluctant for her to get back.

As usual, he had only been trying to spare her the worst. But she had been running from the truth; the truth being that Edward was dead. And she had not even been given the chance to mourn him. Even if she had never loved Edward, he had still been a good friend and had not deserved to die at such a young age. If it was not for him, she was the one who would have died on the spot. It was her lucky day that Edward had been present to bar her ill fate.

Tears flew down her cheeks at the memory of him being stabbed in the back. Thrice. And she still could not forget the shock she had felt at that time. Regrets followed anyway despite her initial reasoning since she could have tried to help him but had instead panicked and had only run for her life.

Now she wished she could turn back time to undo the past. Where she could have at least helped her friend when he had needed her. It was no use mourning over what could have been now. Bygones were bygones and Edward Bigfoot was no longer alive. Memories of her past with Edward flooded her and she smiled nostalgically at some of the good moments they had together. Even if he had been snobbish and a big bore, Kate had grown quite close to him during her engagement with him.

Edward had been unique in his own way. Though he had loved her as deeply as Aidan or Ryce did, he had cared for her to a certain extent.

She still remembered the day he had brought her a cashmere pullover when she was cold.

And it had not been so hard to break of their engagement. Had it been someone else, she would never have dared call off the wedding only two weeks before the actual date. But when she had realized that Aidan was falling in love with her too, she had full trust that Edward would take the news well. And he had.

He had been angry at first; it was all human. But finally they had made up and he had preferred her happiness. It had been the gesture of a true friend and ever since Kate had considered him dear. They had grown to become good friends and Edward had outgrown the crush he had on her. It had been wonderful to be able to connect with him in a way they never had when they had been engaged.

So engrossed was she in her thoughts that she missed the presence behind her and when somebody gagged her mouth, it was too late to even react; forget about freeing herself. Her first reflex was to shout but she could only manage muffled sound as her mouth was stuffed with a cloth. It was so tight that she felt her skin tear against the rough cloth.

This time she did not panic; it was as if she had been bracing herself to face such a situation. She was not even afraid because she knew that this time she would not be spared. The killer was so eager to assassinate her that she knew she would not be spared this time. The proof was that he had not waited for another second to attack again.

As she turned around to see who it was, she felt her head being forcibly held straight ahead and she was unable to veer it. More tears fell as she felt her mouth ache and she tried to shout again but the sound was not even audible to her. Then she felt a veil over her eyes as the world dim around her and all she could see was black.

Pain engulfed her as she felt the pressure against her eyes and she tried hard not to hyperventilate. She knew her time was near and she had to react quickly if she wanted to escape. But she could not move an inch since her body was pinned against a big body and by the force that was being applied on her, she knew it was a man.

And there were only four men who were present here. Her father. Aidan. Ryce. Bryan.

Aidan and her father were out of question. She could trust them with her life. Ryce was also out of question. And suddenly she knew who the killer was. Bryan Stafford.

Kate was at a complete loss why would Bryan want her dead. And that too on her own wedding day? Was he in love with her?! Was that why he was killing her when she was getting married to the love of her life. But it did not make any sense.

She had never picked any vibe from him. Negative or positive. Bryan had blended perfectly well in the Thornton family being the perfect husband to Caitlin and the perfect father to the twins. There was no way he could want to kill her.

Kate would be so sad if it was Bryan. What would happen to Caitlin and the kids? And it was not as if he had done something that he could repent. He was trying to kill her and had already killed someone. There was no going back for whoever it was now and she found herself praying it was not Bryan.

Or was it someone else? Someone who had joined them furtively while their attention had been on Nathalie?

She could be completely wrong; someone else might have followed them like Nathalie had done. It could be Nathalie but she was not strong enough to manhandle her like that. Maybe she had hired someone else to do her dirty job. Yes that made more sense. Because even in her disheveled state, she could not find any reason why her own brother in law would want her dead.

Even in her pain, she tried to focus on the possibilities as she was being forcefully led somewhere. It was not like she had any option than to follow but she was stalling for time by lagging her feet behind. In fact, she was waiting for the killer to make a false move to grab her chance. All the time praying it was not Bryan for the sake of her little innocent nephew and niece.

Then suddenly she realized one thing. What if it was Bryan and what if she did not manage to escape? What if the killer succeeded in his evil intentions where she would end up dead. Would her family live with a murderer like him all their life without knowing his real truth. If it was Bryan, her family would always live in danger; he would not hesitate to kill anyone else for his purpose. Whatever it was.

Feeling some semblance of strength at that thought, she waited until her kidnapper appeared to be close and she kicked around madly and blindly. Thinking of her family, she continuously kicked behind her until she was ruthlessly held against a male body. Damn! She was done for.

Excruciating pain seized her senses as she felt a pressure against her throat. All thoughts stopped as she tried to struggle out of the hold. Damn! She was fighting with all her strength but her attacker was stronger and she was quickly using up all her energy. Trying to keep her wits, she stilled her fight and gasped for air.

It had been a mistake for her to attack when her eyes were blinded. Tears pricked her eyes and she felt in urgent need for air. But there was only the pressure at her throat which was preventing her from breathing in.

When she started to see the black out, by pure reflex, she kicked out once more with not much force but she reached her target. It was square in the groin and her attacker howled in pain. It felt more like her good luck when she suddenly found herself free from any bondage.

For one second, she stood still not believing her good luck, then she got a grip on her senses trying to figure out what to do. Then she broke free from her daze and removed the cover from her eyes. It took her a moment to adjust to the sudden brightness again and when she focused again, she glanced at the form lying down on the ground.

And there he was.

Bryan Stafford. Her own brother-in-law. He was the one trying to kill her. Even if she had doubted that, she still felt shock enter her system as all kinds of thoughts filled her mind. What would happen to her sister? What would happen to the twins? Would they blame her? Was it because of her that everything had started?

But she still could not find any plausible reason why Bryan would want to kill her. Except if she had done something that she knew nothing about. Then she realized that she had to get away again. Without wasting time, she ran towards an arbitrary direction not really having a choice but finally realized that she was lost.

It would seem that when her eyes had been blindfolded, Bryan had dragged her to another place which she could not recognize. But she could not care less; all she wanted was to run. Not only run from the killer. But run from the sordid truth. Run from the truth that the father of her sweet nephews was a killer.

It was like everything was back to square one. She found herself running again on her wedding day except this time she was already married. But it hardly made any difference. Tears blinded her as she picked up speed looking behind her from time to time to see if he was following her.

Thankfully, she had a good advance on him and finally she came to a stop when she could no longer breathe. Hands on her hips, she tried to get back her normal breathing rhythm by taking in deep breath. What was she supposed to do now?

As she scanned around her surroundings, she glanced frantically around but could find only grass. Apparently, Bryan had brought her to a secluded place to finish her. Incensed, she walked on trying to look for civilization where she knew she would be safe. If she found anyone, she knew she could save her skin.

All she wanted to do was contact Aidan and just be with him. If she managed to escape, there was no way she would tell Caitlin that her husband was the one trying to kill her. Her sister would be heart-broken to know the truth.

Tired she finally caught sight of an isolated cottage uphill looking like it was abandoned. Encouraged, she urged her foot to move in that direction when she felt someone pull her from behind and she stumbled down. Afraid, she turned round still in her fallen position to stare at her brother-in-law. And that time she felt another emotion; anger at him and she welcomed it since it gave her some strength.

"Bryan!!" she screamed. "Let me go. Please."

He seemed surprised at her plea and seemed to hesitate for one minute. Then to her utter traumatism, he shook his head and grabbed her by the hair. She winced at the atrocious pain but determined not to give in to him; she tried to maintain a semblance of normality.

"Let me go!" she cried with more force this time than her previous plea.

He shook his head again. "It's too late now. You've seen me. I can't let you go. I'm sorry."

The bastard! He was apologizing before he was forced to kill her? What kind of sadistic logic was that? Kate wanted to slap his face at that moment but she knew she had to calm herself down. Because if she succeeded in rising his wrath, she would be the one bearing the consequences. It was a mistake she had already done. Not again.

"I won't tell anyone. I promise."

He hesitated for some time. Then he shook his head again. She felt her heart sink. Damn! She had to think of something quick.

"I don't understand. Why would you want me dead?" she asked thinking fast. If she got to know of his motive, she would be able to mollify him a bit more. Or buy some time. Aidan and the rest must not be far from where they were since they had walked for only a few minutes. She was sure the others were already looking for her.

But it was her fatal mistake. It looked like she had aroused his anger and she flinched when he tightened his grasp on her hair jerking her head backwards. It was hurting like hell but she played along knowing that the moment of truth was near. Her head was pounding like mad and she was close to a mental breakdown but she knew she had to keep her strength.

Her tenacity was the only thing which would keep her alive eventually.

"You're asking me why?" he hissed. "Nathalie was right. You've been living in a cocoon all your life my darling! Don't tell me you don't know that you have inherited the lion share? Leaving your sisters with only peanuts. And you dare ask me why I'm doing all this?"

Kate was stunned. He was doing all this for money?? The money she had inherited from her father because she had worked hard all her life to deserve? The money she had not even wanted in the end but had believed that nobody wanted it?!! It was crazy.

"Bryan! Are you out of your mind? You are doing this only for money?" she asked unable to mask the emotion in her voice.

"Only for money? Yeah you would say that! You are the spoilt little princess here, aren't you? Have you ever given a thought how we people have to strive for our living? Have you ever realized how unfair it was for you to cash thousands of dollars per month while your sister is being allocated only half of it?"

"But Bryan I work for that money. And I work harder than anyone else. And if Caitlin needed more, all she had to do was ask. I have never refused her anything. And neither had Dad. And besides you're loaded too, aren't you?"

Was that what greed did to a person? Did it blind him to such an extent that it left him with wanting more and more?

"Loaded?" he spat making an evil smile and grabbing her throat with his free hand. Kate screamed at the double pain she was experiencing.

Her headache was already making her feel like she would fall apart anytime. It was difficult for her to maintain her stance now.

"I am bankrupt. I lost all my money on my last business deal. But you're so busy with yourself to notice anything. To notice that your sister has been living like a pauper for the past two years? To notice that my kids are not so privileged anymore?"

Two years? And Kate had never noticed anything. Not even her father had talked to her about that and she had a feeling that nobody knew about her sister's financial crisis. It was a pity and if she had known about it she would have helped Caitlin. Kate was feeling bad for her sister but not or the bastard in front of her.

He had the audacity to explain killing someone like that? If his last business deal had gone wrong, it had been all his own damned fault. And he could have asked for help. Or taken a loan. But killing her or taking up her inheritance was devilish.

"All you had to do was ask for help. Dad would have helped you. I would have helped you. We've never refused you anything. I simply can't believe that you…"

She coughed when she felt a pressure on her throat and she knew she would not be spared. Bryan had already made up his mind; he would kill her. No matter what. But she would never forgive him for what he had done if she was spared. Not even for her sister's sake. Edward was dead because of his crooked mind.

"I don't need your charity dear sister-in-law. Caitlin is your sister and she deserves her share of money as much as you did. Except she's not the favourite daughter and you are not as innocent as you seem. You're going to die; and Caitlin would inherit everything. It's the only way. I will be the owner of Thornton enterprise."

Tears filled her eyes as she felt darkness engulf her senses as she struggled to let in oxygen in her body. There was no going back this time. But just before oblivion took over, she smiled with the knowledge that she was dying as Mrs. Aidan Waldorf. It would seem that her life was not completely wasted after all.

CHAPTER NINETEEN: DEAD OR ALIVE?

A idan felt his blood chill at the sound. It was indistinct, muffled by distance but he could recognize it even when he was dead. It was Kate! Damn! Damn! He could not imagine the plight she must be in. It was only minutes since she had disappeared and Aidan had been looking for her like mad. He vowed not to let anyone harm her a second time.

When Kate had suddenly disappeared, he had tried hard not to panic looking around expecting to find Ryce missing too. But he was perplexed to find his best friend standing beside him looking as worried as hell.

And the only person missing had been Bryan Stafford. Oh holy shit! Ryce had nodded in his direction to confirm his doubt. It was the brother-in-law who had concocted such a conspiracy. No time to feel remorse for having doubted his best friend, they had immediately started to give each other instructions which way to go.

But not before asking Alex to stay with the rest of the women in the cottage. Nobody had guessed what was going on thankfully and now he feared the worst. Bryan would not spare Kate; not this second time.

Then he heard the sound again. Let me go! It was easier to discern now which told him that he was going in the right direction. Nearer to Kate; he just hoped he reached on time so that he could help her. His heart was as heavy as lead and he found it difficult to draw in his normal breath. Heaven knew what would happen to his Katie this time.

Finally, he caught sight of some movement not far across a deserted hill and without thinking he dashed towards the isolated place. And what he saw made his heart stop beating.

Bryan was holding Kate by her throat and she looked as pale as a ghost shaking with the effort to draw in a breath. The sight broke Aidan but he knew that he was dealing with a relentless murderer and he had to tread stealthily. However, he was unprepared for the third person already present there as he approached nearer.

There was Caitlin standing two feet away pointing a gun in the direction of Kate and his heart screamed at the sight. Without taking a moment to breathe, he dived in between the two sisters ready to take the bullet in the place of Kate. It would have been a perfect timing too had someone not pulled him from behind at the last second.

It was Ryce.

"Aidan!! What the hell are you doing?" his friend exclaimed getting up and extending a hand to help him get up.

But Aidan had no time to reply him. He leaned on the support to stand up and looked back at the body which laid slumped on the ground and he rushed to it feeling like it was the worst moment of his life. Kate had been shot by her own sister. Tears filled his vision and he vowed that if something happened to Kate, he would never ever be the same again.

Life would just end for him. As he rushed by the side of his beloved blinded by tears, he picked up the lifeless body unable to bear the pain. Kate was not responding and he was shaking her feeling desperate. He could no longer hear what was going on around him. All he cared about was his wife who laid lifeless in his arms and he wanted her back.

"Aidan!!!" Ryce was shouting. "Aidan, please control yourself."

Aidan looked up at his friend without actually seeing anything. And he was not reacting; not until Ryce forcefully took Kate from his arms that he realized what was happening around him.

"What are you doing?" he screamed snapping out of his daze and watching Ryce cuddling his beloved in his arms.

"She's alive. She needs medical attention. Get a grip!" Ryce rasped and at the same time Alex joined them rushing towards them on seeing the lifeless Kate. Her father bent to feel her pulse and confirmed that she was alive although somewhat weak.

It was then that Aidan realized that the bullet had hit Bryan and not Kate. Caitlin had aimed at her husband to protect her sister. Aidan had completely misunderstood the situation and had freaked out when he had seen Caitlin pointing a gun towards them. She had been aiming her husband and that was why Ryce had saved him. Bryan was lying on the floor with blood pooling around his body and Caitlin was down on her knees crying her heart out.

Aidan felt pity for her; it must have been hard for her to choose between her husband and her sister irrespective of how the husband was. But he was glad that she was not part of the conspiracy. It would have killed Kate if Caitlin had tried to kill her for money. Aidan was the only person who knew how little money counted for Kate.

Alex seemed to have picked up the situation moved towards his other daughter and kicked the pistol out of reach. Then he picked up the shell shocked Caitlin who was still crying like it was the end of the world. It was a heart wrenching scene but his attention was diverted as he heard a small coughing sound in his right. It was where Ryce was standing coming from Kate.

He rushed to her side at the first sign of life everything else forgotten. "Kate..."

"Aiiiiidan," she whispered weakly. And coughed again this time more roughly and he caressed her back while Ryce put her down on a nearby patch of grass.

"What happened?" she asked again and tried to get up when she saw Caitlin in the arms of her father. "Where's Bryan?"

Aidan shushed and asked her how she felt. The skin at her throat was rash and looked terribly sensitive. He wanted to caress it but he feared he might hurt her more. She looked frail and weak and Aidan wanted to take her to the hospital for medical attention.

But he knew how Kate were. It was going to be difficult to convince her to attend herself when her sister was in such a bad plight. And he was right. As soon as Kate caught sight of the depressed version of Caitlin, she sat up pushing away any support he was offering.

"Caitlin," she cried walking to her. "I'm so sorry."

Aidan had to suppress his concern for her which was not quite settling down with him. Not after he had seen his wife almost dead only a few minutes ago.

Why the hell was she apologizing? Wasn't her sister the one who should apologize for having such a lousy husband? Aidan knew he was being insensitive but all he cared about was that Kate at that moment. At her words, Caitlin stopped crying, sobbed once or twice but did not say anything. Kate's face was filled with guilt and Aidan feared that she was blaming herself for what had happened. He did not know how but he was sure it was some warped female logic again.

And he was starting to grow tired of all the drama. Every second there was something new which came up and he was not able to cope anymore. Just as he was looking for a way to cut off the drama that he was sure was going to trigger, there was a click sound in the air.

Everybody froze as the sound resounded through the silent scenery. Aidan saw Bryan who had gotten up when nobody was looking and had picked up the gun. Blood was oozing out of his left arm and Aidan had not thought to check where he had been hit. Damn!

But his game was over now. It would serve him no purpose to kill Kate now. There was no way Alex would make him the successor now that his true nature was out. However with the turn of events,

Aidan could never be sure. So he moved towards Kate to protect her but Bryan pointed the gun in his direction.

"Don't move!"

"Okay!" he replied promptly. "Please don't shoot," he begged. He did not want anybody harmed. "Don't shoot," he repeated lifting his hands up as guise of surrender. He was not that stupid to endanger the lives of so many people around. But he remained alert in case Bryan got mad and decided to shoot after all.

"Bryan!" said Caitlin. "What are you doing?"

At the sound of his wife's voice, Bryan stopped in his flight and looked back at where Caitlin stood with her father. "I'm sorry. I have to go. It's too late for me to revert back. I already killed someone and I will not be acquitted."

Caitlin gasped at his confession. And Aidan noticed that the other ladies had joined them too. Jade and June stood shocked while the Bigfoots looked angry.

"Why did you kill my son? What did he do?" asked Abigail speaking for the first time ever since she had joined them.

"I had no choice. I wanted to kill Kate but he was at the wrong place at the wrong time," Bryan said laughing dryly. "It was his bad luck," he shrugged.

"You mean to say that I lost my son for a petty reason?" Abigail whispered in a low voice and Judith came from behind to support her friend. There was no comfort for them. What was done was done. Edward Bigfoot was no more because he had been the sacrificial lamb in some sort of way.

"Bryan, please stop!" pleaded Caitlin. "You can still repent. Think of the twins. Stop this madness for their sake. Please surrender to the police. I will wait for you. I promise. "

"Police? Never!! I will never spend my life in jail. Never. Do you hear me my dear wife?" Bryan shouted pointing the gun towards Caitlin and Alex now. "You are nothing what I thought you were. I thought you were a rich heiress when I married you. But you are nothing but a pale copy of your wonderful sister here!"

And Aidan gasped as he pointed the gun towards Kate again.

"How dare you!" shouted Caitlin. "How dare you say that you've married me for money and insult us in the same breath? You bastard!"

Aidan felt Ryce move and he knew that the latter was thinking along the same line as himself. It was futile trying to provoke Bryan when he had a gun. He could shoot someone anytime and it would be fatal. Instead, they should try to calm him down so that once he put the gun down it would be less dangerous.

"I would have kept you happy. You would never have known. But you were too busy playing the good sister instead of trying to help me out. I wanted so much for both of us but you spoiled everything Caitlin. Look at what you made me do."

"I didn't! I am not responsible for your actions. I always supported you even during the financial problems. Except that you expected me to tell my father about your failings. It's not fair that he should be the one to cover up for your sorry ass."

"And it's fair that he should cover the failings of your elder sister? What about all the money that is being given to her?"

"Bryan, listen." It was Kate. She had spoken for the first time and her voice was still husky but some of her original color was back in her face. "I will give you everything I have. Every penny. Please put the gun down. Please."

It was so typical of Kate. She was the one generous enough to forgive him for all the misery her brother-in-law had inflicted on her for the sake of her sister.

"You will?" Bryan asked finally as if someone was getting to her.

"Yes. But you will have to surrender to the police. If you do so, I will transfer all my property in your name," Kate told him getting nearer to him.

No, no, no Kate. Don't do that. Aidan wanted to grab her but finally she stopped and Aidan realized that she had walked away from her sister and father so that if Bryan had a shot at her, the two would be spared. It was so clever of her but so foolish at the same time. What if she had flustered Bryan in the process. The latter was already freaking out as it was.

"No, no. I will never go to jail. You will have to forget the little incident and I will be ready to forgive you for all that you have done," her brother-in-law replied back almost spatting the words as he spoke.

Wait a damn second! Bryan was being so magnanimous! He was the one ready to forgive Kate for having the gall to try to kill her. It was the world upside down, really. He wished Kate would not accept that he was to be forgiven. There was no way they could tolerate such a murderer in their family now that they've known the truth.

"Okay. Whatever you say," gave in Kate and Aidan knew that she was doing everything for her sister's sake.

And suddenly he guessed what Kate was trying to do. She was trying to make him out the gun down so that nobody else would be killed again. That was why she was agreeing to his every condition. He wished nobody protested as it would only spoil the game. But unfortunately, not everyone was as brilliant as his newly wedded wife.

"Kate!! Are you ready to forgive him for what he did to my son?" interrupted Abigail. "How can you do that?"

Damn that woman! He wished somebody would signal her that Kate was only trying to cajole Bryan so that he would put the gun down. Once he did that, then Ryce and himself would pounce on him like two predators. But apparently Abigail was so pent up with emotions that she was not able to see what Kate was trying to do. But Aidan could understand her plight; she had just discovered the killer of her son and it must not be easy for her to digest the fact that Edward was gone only because of a big mistake.

"Mrs. Bigfoot. I'm sorry but Bryan is family," Kate said trying desperately to send her a warning look in her direction.

But Bryan seem to catch her look and he cursed loudly. "You're playing me for a fool, you stupid bitch! I'm not wasting my time with you."

And with that, he rushed in the direction of the cottage and Aidan deduced he was heading towards the car. Damn! They had to get to him before he got away. Without wasting time, Aidan dashed after him closely followed by Ryce ready to confront him now that the whole family was safe.

However, when they reached, he was already starting the white Rolls Royce and Aidan found the car keys missing in the other two cars.

Damn! Damn! Damn! Bryan had managed to fool them. He was so clever that he had taken the two car keys before he took the fastest car. It was impossible for them to go after him now.

"Damn! He got away!" muttered Ryce looking as frustrated as he was feeling. And at that precise moment, Aidan felt so guilty to have doubted him in the first place. He was so glad to have an ally in such a situation. He decided to tell him the truth.

"Ryce I thought it was you who was trying to kill Kate."

"What?!!" Ryce asked him staring at him like he had grown two heads. "Why the hell would I kill Kate? I love her as much as you do," he protested.

"I know! I must have been out of my mind trying to figure out who was behind all this. I'm sorry bro; we had such a history that I thought you were still not in good terms with what happened. I'm really sorry," he apologized. He vowed never to doubt Ryce again. He was the brother he never had. It was official.

"Never mind that. I know it has not been easy for you. Go find your wife; I'll call the police to send them after Bryan's trail."

Aidan nodded and rushed back to the hill where the others were still gathered. Once he reached, he saw Kate and Caitlin hugging and he deduced that the two sisters had made peace. It was a relief to find that Caitlin held no grudge against her sister but he knew it was going to be difficult for her to manage the twins.

Life was a bitch sometimes. Caitlin was the sweetest person on earth and she so did not deserve such a terrible fate. Feeling bad for having doubted her too, he moved towards the two enlaced sisters.

"Where's he?" Caitlin asked him as soon as she caught sight of him. Even in the worst situation, she was still worried about her husband. What a pity that the man was such a vile character. It was not going to be easy to oust him out of their lives despite the villainous role he had played. Bryan Stafford had been accepted as part as the Thornton family.

Aidan shook his head not really knowing how to disclose the news. "He got away."

Kate gasped. Caitlin closed her eyes. Whether in relief or pain, Aidan could not make out. It was such a complicated situation for her.

Bryan looked unwilling to surrender himself to the police and there was no way they could accept him back for what he had done. Not after having already committed a murder and still not even repenting for it.

"I can't believe it. We have been suffering from money problems for the past two years but I thought it was okay. I mean I would have stayed with him anyway. Even if he was poor. But lately he had been pestering me to talk to Dad about our state. Especially since he knew that Kate had inherited the company. I never thought that…"

She faltered and Kate squeezed her arms. "Nobody thought that he would do something like that. Hell, if I had known, I would have given him the money."

"Nooo, it's your money. You worked hard for it. I know how much you've studied and worked for that. It would have been so unfair for my husband to take everything from you. And I don't think I would have liked to live with such a person."

Aidan was so glad that Caitlin was not taking the side of her husband. It took a strong woman to be able to think rationally in the toughest times. But she was the only one who knew what was going on in her head at that moment.

"You're right Caitlin," her father intervened. "If he had tried to embezzle my money or something I would have forgiven him. But he had tried to kill, be it Edward or Kate. I can never forgive him for that. And I don't think anybody can forgive him that. It would not be fair to Edward. He was part of the family too."

"True," said Judith still supporting her friend. It was sad that Edward had left them for absolutely no valid reason. Such a loss for nothing. "By God's grace, we are still able to look after Caitlin rather than to leave her in the hands of such a murderer. She's better off without him."

All things said, Caitlin burst into tears again and everybody comforted her again. It was easier said than done. It was going to be a tough fight; fight against life but as Aidan stood to watch the undying support around her, he was sure that she would survive anything. Or at least he hoped so.

EPILOGUE: FINALLY YOURS...

SOME MONTHS LATER.....

"Have you any news of him today?" asked Kate as soon as he got home. It was becoming a habit now. Every evening it was the first question his lovely wife asked him. Before she even asked her how was his day.

Kate had recovered from her minor injuries and he was thankful that she had managed to escape the evil intention of Bryan Stafford. Aidan knew it was something that was bothering her. The fact that her brother-in-law was still out there somewhere. But he did not believe he was a threat anymore. He had wanted money and he knew there was no way he would get a single penny from them now.

"No. The police are still looking for him. But frankly it's been a while now and I'm sure they will drop the search. Bryan is a clever man and he would never dare show his face again. Stop worrying about him and come kiss me," he said smiling at her.

Without waiting to be asked twice, she ran in her arms and he had to brace himself against the impact. He grinned.

"Now that's so much better for a welcome. So what have you been up to today?" he asked kissing her playfully on the nose. Kate was not working. Alex had banned her from office since the past week. And Aidan had approved.

After their honeymoon, she had been working like a machine and had fainted in the office once or twice. Alex had taken the matters seriously and had asked her to take a few weeks off. Of course she had protested but her family could be a remarkable army when affronted and Kate had no other choice than to give in meekly.

Aidan had been over the moon especially when he had discovered that Kate had occupied her free time by starting to write a book. Writing, Aidan had discovered over the last week was her passion. There was not a situation or a moment where she did not come up with poems and rhythms.

Sometimes, he would be in an important conference call and Kate would send him the sweetest and most romantic words ever which would make his heart melt all over again. And made him want to leave everything behind and go to her. Sometimes he resisted but most of the times it was too hard for him to resist her.

"I've already figured out the story so far. I have started on chapter one today," she told him. "Would you like to read it?"

Damn! Did he have to? He was such a lousy reader normally but romantic novels were really not his cup of tea. Hell the last time he had read a book, it had taken him six months to finish it and by that time, he had already forgotten what happened in the first chapters!!

Trying not to disappoint her, he smiled and removed his mobile to quickly change the subject. "I have got something for you. It's a surprise," he said winking at her.

"Really? What it is?" she asked gleefully thankfully forgetting the reading part.

"Here," he said showing her the screen of his mobile. "Here is a community of writers. There are so many talented readers and writers on this website. Try having a look and I think you should post your work as well."

Kate felt happy that he had bothered to look for something so important for her. It was something she had been wishing to do for herself for a long time but life had always caught up with her. Now living in

Brooklyn with Aidan, life was much quieter as she was handling the Brooklyn branch.

Caitlin had joined office to start handling the Manhattan office and Judith was the happiest grandmother on earth babysitting her two wonderful grandsons. Kate was glad that she also had the time to write now. It had been something she had used to do during her teens and she had never realized how much she had missed writing.

She was a natural, she had found out but she had never dared shown anyone her work before. Except one poem she had written for Aidan years ago. But now that Aidan had offered her the opportunity to connect with some of her fellow writers, she could not help feeling nervous about what others would think of her work.

It was Aidan who had encouraged her to start writing. One day she had woken up and had narrated a story to him; a story which had been trotting in her mind for a long time now. Aidan had found in interesting and after he had helped her with some of the loopholes, he had urged her to start on her new project.

Kate had been excited and it was the seventh time she had asked Aidan to read what she had written so far. But she knew reading bored him to death. She did not mind really. Guys were usually so slow sometimes.

And besides, he did help her in his own way. Like he had now by looking for the writers' community to help her share her work and she might get an opinion if she was really that good.

"Hmm let me see," she said glancing at his screen. "Wattpad. I've never heard of it before. Thank you so much for helping me doing something like that," she told him sincerely. "I've got a surprise for you too," she told him.

"Yah?" he asked. "Now what more could you offer me sweetheart?"

Without replying, she took his hand and placed his right palm on her belly. Aidan felt confused for a second and then realization kicked in. She was showing him her belly. Her belly!! Which meant only one thing. She was pregnant.

The joy must have been evident on his face because she laughed and she did not even have to confirm it. Of course! That was the reason why she had been fainting in the office. Aidan had taken her to a doctor for general checkup last Monday and she must have gotten her reports today.

Hell, he was going to be a father. It was the happiest moment of his life and he could not stop his grin. "How many months?"

"Two and a half," she said happily. "I'm so happy love."

"Me too," he laughed lifting her up in his arms and whirling her round in glee. "You've made me the happiest man Kate. You are the best thing that happened to me. And to think I would have let you go because of my damned ego," he mused putting her down in case she might be giddy.

"Oh it would have been impossible honey," she told him confidently and kissed him on the mouth savouring the kiss.

"Oh and why is that?" he asked puzzled at her cocky attitude.

"Because I was always meant to be yours....."

It was so truly said. She was such a poet at heart. Whatever happened in life, she would have always came back to him. She belonged to him as much as he belonged to her. They were simply destined to end up together. It was what was meant to be.

****